Nature's Patterns

Inspirations and Techniques for Quilt Makers

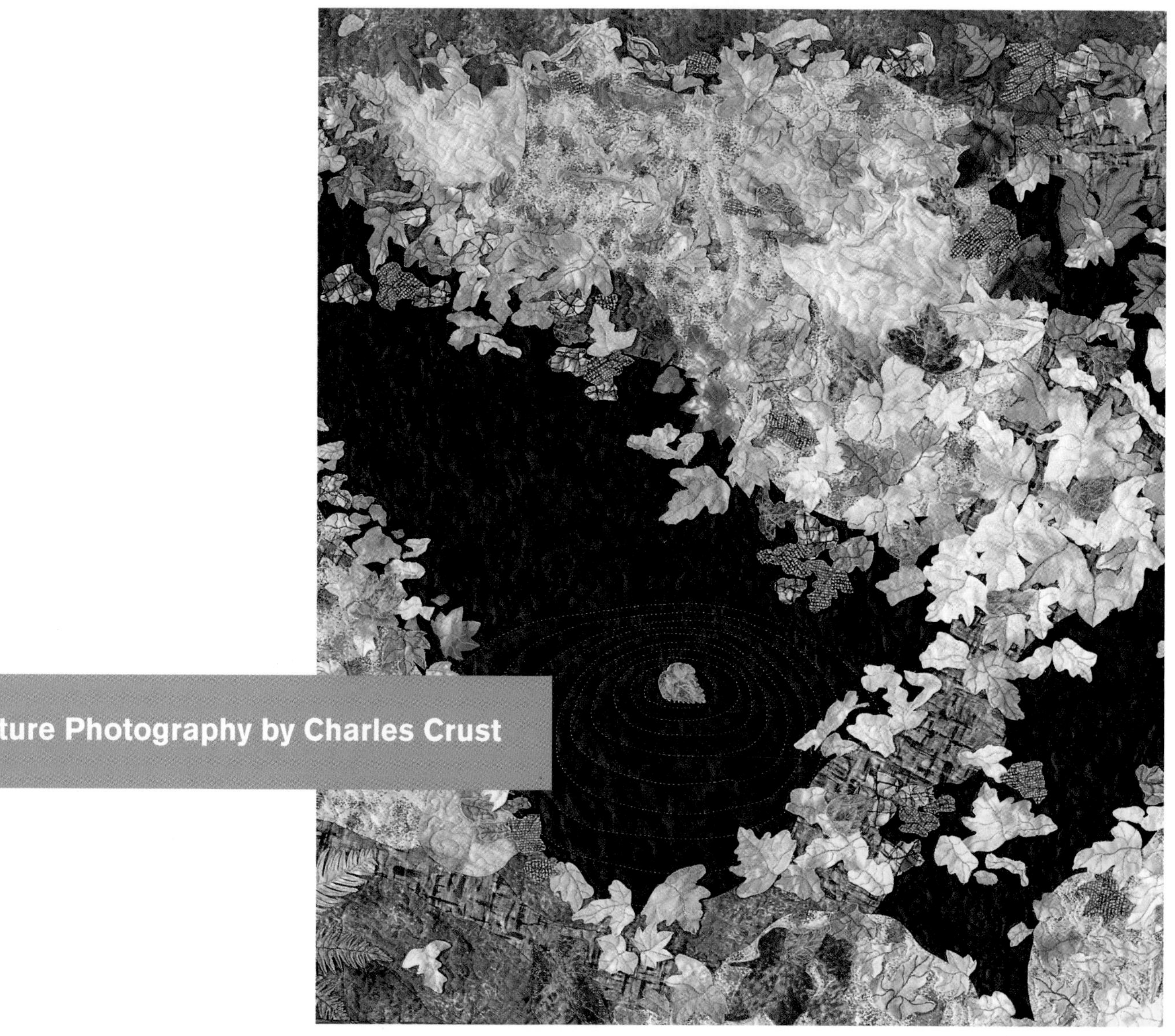

Nature Photography by Charles Crust

Joyce R. Becker

Nature's Patterns

THE QUILT DIGEST PRESS
Simply the Best from NTC Publishing Group
Lincolnwood, Illinois U.S.A.

Editorial and production direction by Anne Knudsen.
Book and cover design by Kajun Graphics.
Technical editing by Kandy Petersen.
Technical drawings by Kandy Petersen.
Copyediting by Janet Reed.
Nature photography by Charles Crust.
Quilt photography by Sharon Risedorph, San Francisco.
Printed in Hong Kong.

Library of Congress Cataloging-in-Publication Data

Becker, Joyce R.
Nature's patterns : inspirations and techniques for quilt makers
Joyce R. Becker.
p. cm.
ISBN 0-8442-2648-3
1. Quilting—Patterns. 2. Nature (Aesthetics) I. Title.
TT835.B43 1996
746.46—dc20 95-38016
CIP

1997 Printing

Published by The Quilt Digest Press
a division of NTC Publishing Group
4255 West Touhy Avenue
Lincolnwood (Chicago), IL 60646-1975, U.S.A.

6 7 8 9 0 WKT 9 8 7 6 5 4 3 2

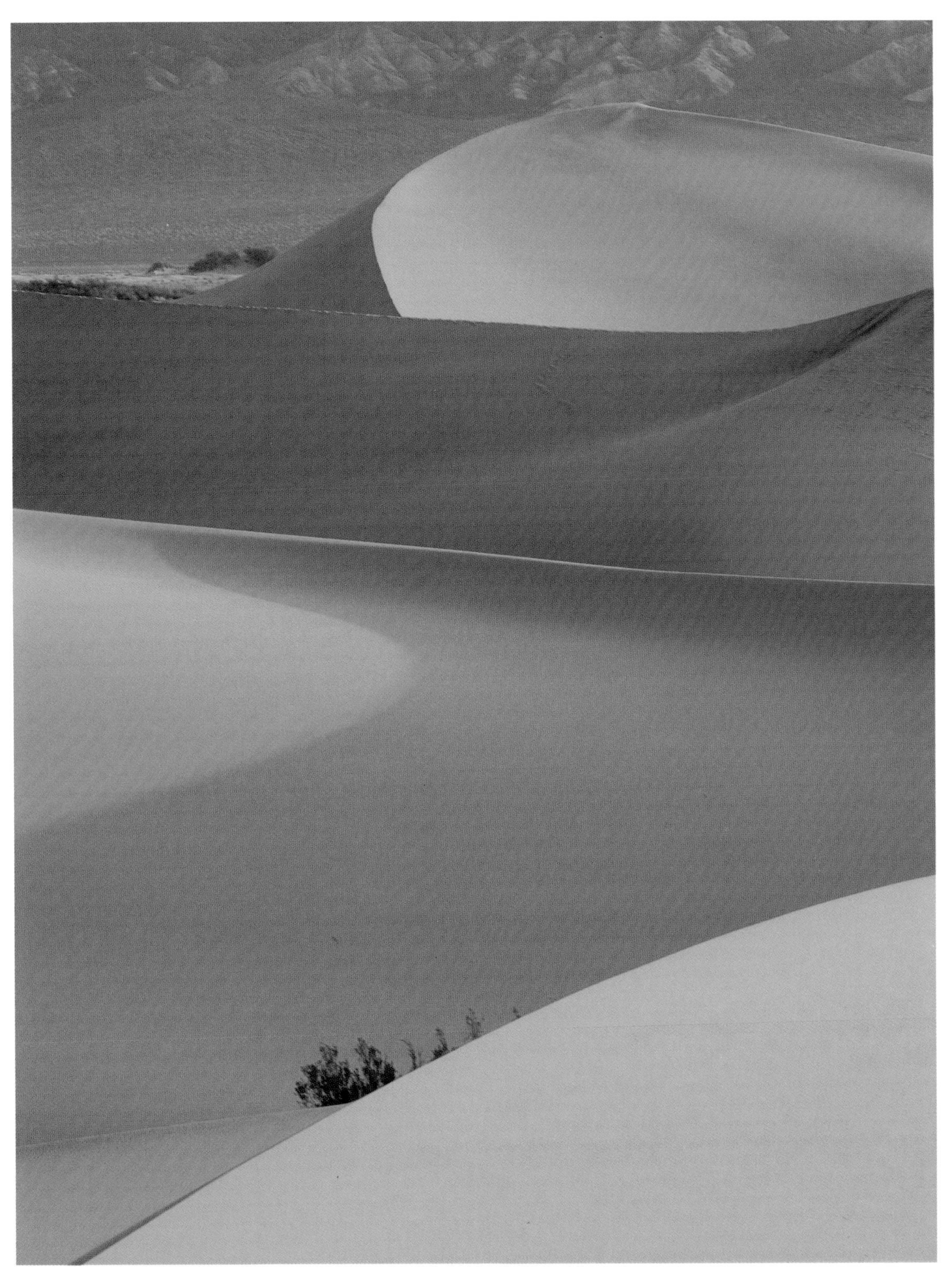

To Donald, for accepting me for who I am.

Contents

Introduction

LOOKING BACK over my love affair with quilts, I still find myself charged with electricity when I come upon one that possesses the uncanny ability to speak to me. My first impulse is to wrap myself in it and revel in the comforting cotton that carries me back through the decades, connecting me with those throughout history who have created quilts. Then I find myself studying it, mesmerized by its movement of design and color.

The awesome beauty of nature has long inspired quilt artists: the grace of a bird effortlessly soaring through the clouds or the sight of fresh snow weighing down the boughs of an evergreen. Such images make their way into quilts that come alive, surging and pulsating with emotion, or reflect quiet peace, bringing the warmth and tranquility of a spring day when budding flowers awaken, their dewy petals heavy with the fragrance of new life. In capturing even a fraction of this inspiration in their quilts, artists complete the circle back to nature.

Certain people provide great inspiration simply by believing in both their creativity and ours. All of the quilt artists I have chosen for this book have this gift. They have captured the untamed seduction of nature and translated their visions into spectacular works. Because I have often wanted to know the inspiration behind a particular quilt and where the passion came from during the creation process, it seems vital to include personal reflections from the artists. We will tiptoe through their minds so you, too, can experience their creative energies and, in the process, discover the common bond that weaves itself through each work, connecting quilters everywhere.

My fondest wish is that you will use this book as a catalyst to open your mind and soul to nature 's inspirations. Start with a pattern and adapt it to include the colors and textures that exist in your particular surroundings. Use this book as a tool to perfect your techniques, then move on to design your own quilts. We often choose the safest route on the path of creativity, following published patterns and designs. Consider veering off the safe path and venturing into the unknown. You may encounter unexpected turns along your trek, but the end result will not only demonstrate your creativity, it will also give you permission to grow and expand as an artist. Those who have taken that leap of faith and embarked on original design quilts agree that discovery resulted only after they lost their fear of failure or the unknown.

Nature 's inspiration surrounds you, even if you live in a city. Look at the sprinkling of clouds on the horizon at sunset, kissed with just a hint of pink before the sun disappears. Imagine sunlight streaming through the branches of an old oak tree, creating shadows as leaves crackle with energy. Fly with what you see, create something that is truly yours, that expresses your unique view. Look around, you will be amazed at the possibilities.

Come with me now on an exciting exploration of the ever changing mystery and moods of nature and catch a glimpse into the minds of its quilt artists.

How to Use *Nature's Patterns*

Each theme-based chapter of the book opens with a beautiful scenic photograph by Charles Crust that represents the inspiration of the quilts that follow. For each quilt, you will find a full photograph, some information regarding the techniques used, a profile of the quilt artist, and a brief passage on the artist's specific inspiration. We have included instructions for about two-thirds of the quilts to help you get started. The others, generally more whimsical creations, have been added to facilitate your imagination. Remember, anything is possible.

If you are unfamiliar with the techniques used by the artists, I invite you to refer to some of the books published by The Quilt Digest Press. These wonderful references will answer your technical questions regarding the construction process of most quilts. These are listed in the Resources section.

All directions include a 1/4″ seam allowance unless otherwise stated. When appropriate, templates or illustrations have been provided. Most of these patterns are geared for beginning to intermediate quilters. Since the underlying theme of this book emphasizes individuality and growth and most of the quilts pictured are one-of-a-kind art quilts, the artists have furnished fabric and cutting instructions only for their finished size rather than for various sizes. Many of the artists used specific products to create their particular work of art. When possible, these products are listed in the Resources section at the back of the book.

Acknowledgments

I WILL BE FOREVER GRATEFUL to Bill Folk, former publisher of The Quilt Digest Press, for understanding my vision for this book and for guiding, molding, and stretching my concept to a higher plane. My thanks to James Nelson as well for his direction and valuable input. I am grateful to NTC Publishing Group and Executive Editor, Anne Knudsen, for seeing this book through and for carrying on the quality tradition of The Quilt Digest Press.

Bonnie Miller, thank you for being my writing mentor. Pat Michelsen, you are a true friend, and I deeply appreciate your proofreading my original book proposal. Thank you, Charles Crust, for your patience, your willingness to change directions midstream, and most of all, your photographic genius. Melanie Crossett Duyungan, you have been a godsend. Thank you for helping me pull this book together and being my "assistant." Special thanks to Ros Rowley-Penk and Sylvia Jacobus for pattern testing and proofing. Without my quilting friends, my guild, The Evergreen Piecemakers, and my new quilting friends from The Association of Pacific Northwest Quilters, this book would never have happened. You have filled an important space in my life, and I thank you.

I would also like to thank my family for encouragement, especially Charlotte for cajoling me back into the writing profession. Thank you to my parents for instilling drive and spirit early on. And to my husband, Donald, my stepchildren, our sons, Shawn and Shane, thank you for your love and support. My undying gratitude to the quilt artists in this book who so graciously provided their art and opened their souls without complaint. To all of you listed, thank you for believing in me and my vision.

Quilt Artists

Joyce R. Becker
Flo Burghardt
Rosy Carolan
Sheila R. Chapman
Melody Crust
Patti Cunningham
Karen Schoepflin Hagen
Karla Harris
Elizabeth Hendricks
Jane Herbst
Connie James
Jeanne Nelson Loy
Kathy Martin
Ree Nancarrow
Kathleen M. O'Hanlon
Barbara Lee Olson
Karen Perrine
Charlene Phinney
Roslyn Rowley-Penk
Brenda Duncan Shornick
Heather W. Tewell
Ivy Tuttle
Deborah White

CHAPTER 1 *Electrifying Palettes*

Dawn lights a red and yellow tulip field, Skagit Valley, WA.

Garden Path
Brenda Duncan Shornick
74″ x 95″ (188 cm x 241 cm)
Machine pieced, hand quilted, nine patch and log cabin variation

Garden Path

I LIKE THE CONNECTION quilting provides across generations and cultures. Even though abilities and choices vary, the connection remains. Quilting is an artistic outlet for so many people, and the wonderful thing is that there's room for everybody. Anything that is an expression is art. Taking something, like a feeling, and translating it into something you can see is art. The important part of creating art is the doing, the process, not the end result.

Color can be intimidating to some people, and they can spend a lot of time agonizing over their color choices. The one thing I have learned from nature is color courage. When buying fabric, I try to keep nature's inspiration in mind.

I think about an idea for a new quilt for a long time and mull it around, refining the design before I begin. When I shop for fabrics, my original quilt plan often vanishes because I see other fabrics and colors I want to use. I always arrange my colors on the wall to see how they work together. This part is very exciting to me. Then I make myself become disciplined and sew my quilt together. I think quilting techniques are like vocabulary: The more you do, the more you can do. If there's anything that improves your art, it is you. You need to experiment and realize it's okay if something doesn't turn out the way you had hoped. Give yourself permission to get in there and cut up fabric. You won't be disappointed because you've learned to value the process as well as the end product.

Brenda Duncan Shornick

INSPIRATION

Brenda enjoys making quilts from traditional designs using brightly colored, contemporary fabrics. In this quilt, she wanted to embrace the rich and vibrant color palette of mixed bouquets of northwestern flowers, emphasizing obvious value differences. Rather than strip piecing her design, repeating the same floral prints and combinations throughout, Brenda selectively shopped and cut individual pieces of fabric so the eye flows over the quilt, seeing a real mixed bouquet.

When coming up with the actual placement of her blocks, Brenda hoped to impart a happy or warm feeling, so she moved them about, pondering their placement. At first, her design did not speak to her. She walked away to give her design time to jell, and when she returned to her working wall, she moved and turned her blocks around again. Suddenly her inner voice said, "Yes, this is exactly what I wanted." Listening to that voice and letting your design speak to you is a crucial part of successful quilt art.

It is certainly feasible to strip piece the nine patch designs, using a variety of two inch strips, but the diversity of the floral prints cut individually certainly add to the charm and overall appeal of this work.

TECHNIQUE

10½″ x 10½″ (26.7 cm x 26.7 cm) block

Fabric Suggestions and Requirements

Choose multicolored florals in medium to large scale prints, the more selections the better. This quilt contains 150 different fabrics. When purchasing fabric, buy ⅛ yard (11 cm) to ¼ yard (23 cm) each of 50 dark and 50 light fabrics. High contrast between lights and darks is important.

Blocks
4½ yards (412 cm) light fabrics
5 yards (457 cm) dark fabrics

Inside Border
½ yard (46 cm) pieced

Outside Border
3 yards (274 cm) unpieced

Cutting

Nine Patch Blocks
Cut 240—2″ (5.1 cm) dark squares
Cut 192—2″ (5.1 cm) light squares

Logs
Cut 2—1½″ (3.8 cm) strips from each fabric.
You may need to cut more as blocks progress.

Inside Border
Cut 1¼″ (3.2 cm) wide

Outside Border
Cut 5½″ (14 cm) wide

Instructions

Make 48 nine patch blocks. Alternate light and dark squares. Refer to diagram 1 for piecing order.

Make 47 Block A's. Add log strips to each nine patch center block, going around all four sides three times. See diagram 2 for light and dark placement.

Make 1 Block B using dark fabric for three sides, and light fabric for one side. See diagram 3 for light and dark placement.

Assembly

Assemble your quilt in rows of six blocks across and eight blocks down. Sew blocks into rows; join rows.

Sew inside and outside borders together. Attach borders to quilt top, miter the corners. See diagram 4.

Quilting

Hand or machine quilt as desired.

Note: The nine patch blocks could be made using conventional strip piecing methods if you do not mind repeating fabrics. Refer to *Quilts! Quilts!! Quilts!!!* listed in Resources for this option.

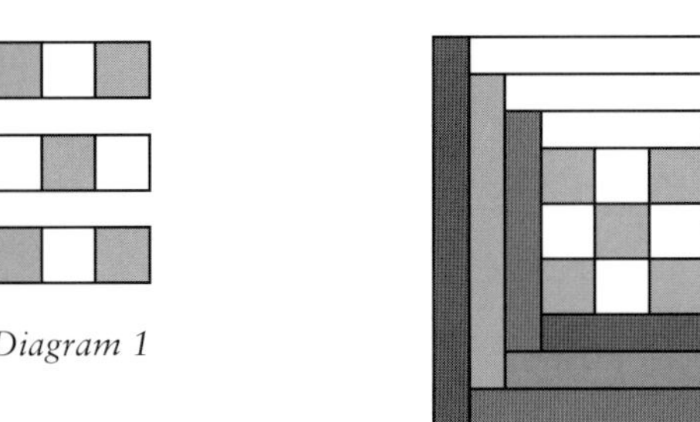

Diagram 1

BLOCK A
Diagram 2

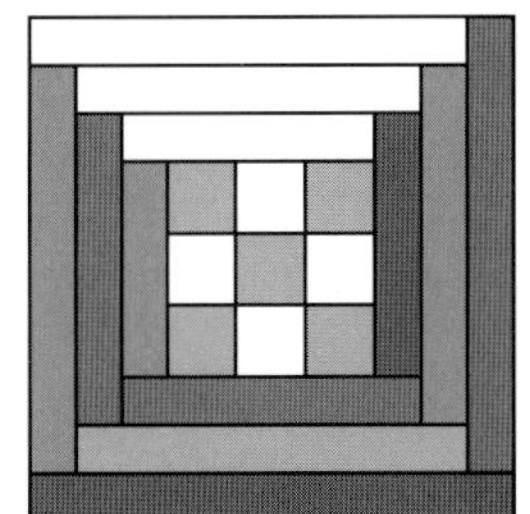

BLOCK B
Diagram 3

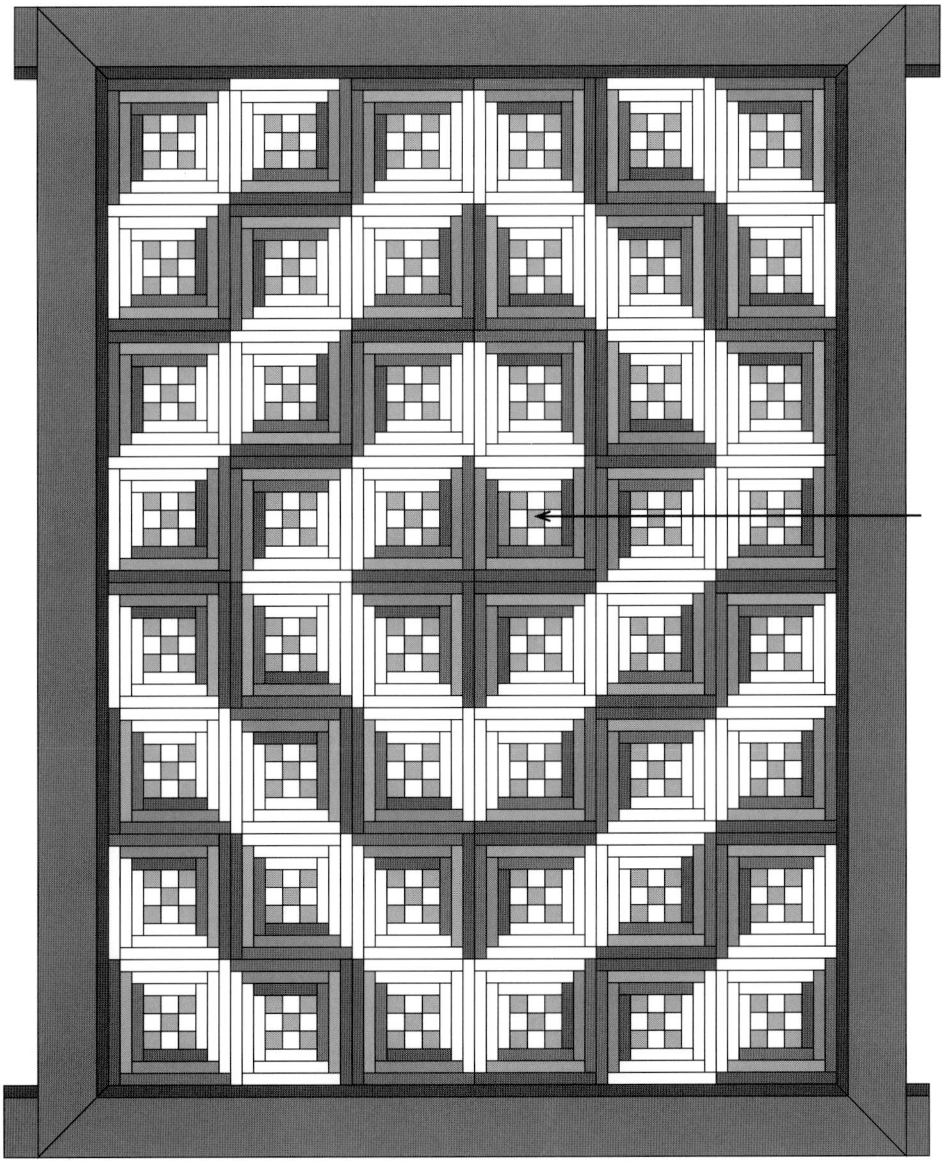

BLOCK B

Diagram 4

Memories of Ben
Jeanne Nelson Loy
44″ x 44″ (112 cm x 112 cm)
Hand appliquéd and quilted

Memories of Ben

As long as I can look forward to seeing one of my designs created tomorrow, I don't dwell on the negative aspects of life. Quilt making makes me optimistic and keeps me going, resulting in my good health.

I find real satisfaction in designing and making quilts inspired by nature. I carefully place my leaves or flowers into positions you would find outdoors. I find warmth in what nature does with color, so I generally use such colors. I try to visualize the best color choices for my nature inspired quilts and use fabrics that fit the design. I also find that looking in the rearview mirror of my car helps isolate designs. It allows me to focus or frame a specific scene for a quilt.

When I see the design come together, I get very excited. When I create quilts, I like to have what I call a permanent photo, done on cloth, of what's in my mind. I sketch my idea first, then I figure out the dimensions, and then I select fabrics. I try to follow high quality standards in my techniques when I am assembling my quilts. Time is not an element because I find quilt making both relaxing and enjoyable.

I like to challenge myself with my quilt art, and I want to do things that my peers will enjoy. I appreciate it when I have learned a lesson by striving for my goal, but I primarily make my art to please myself.

Jeanne Nelson Loy

INSPIRATION

This quilt is a tribute to Jeanne's father, Ben Nelson, of Suquamish, Washington. Ben had a true love for rhododendrons and devoted every spare hour introducing and breeding new varieties, studying the flowers, and then sharing his knowledge with anyone who would listen. According to Jeanne, "My father was an encouraging and enthusiastic teacher, and I just wanted to share my appreciation of his contribution and continue his enjoyment of the flower with this quilt."

The wonderful thing about this quilt is the fact that it could be made with a variety of flowers. Jeanne suggests you create your own regional flowers and leaves for this pattern; anything with a floret will work.

TECHNIQUE

9″ x 9″ (22.8 cm x 22.8 cm) blocks

Fabric Requirements

Sky
3/4 yard (69 cm) hand-dyed light blue/white

Woods
3/4 yard (69 cm) dark fabric

Florets
1 yard (91 cm) or more depending on size and placement of flowers in print

Leaves
1/2 yard (46 cm)

Narrow Border
1/4 yard (23 cm)

Sashing and Outer Border
1 1/2 yards (137 cm)

Cutting

Sky
Cut 4—9 1/2″ (24.1 cm) squares
Cut 1—9 7/8″ (25.1 cm) square, cut in half diagonally

Woods
Cut 3—9 1/2″ (24.1 cm) squares
Cut 1—9 7/8″ (25.1 cm) square, cut in half diagonally

Florets
Cut selected areas of floral fabric using template

Leaves
Cut leaves in a variety of sizes using templates

Narrow Borders
Cut 2—1 1/4″ (3.2 cm) wide

Sashing
Cut 6—1 1/2″ x 11″ (3.8 cm x 27.9 cm)
Cut 2—1 1/2″ x 34″ (3.8 cm x 86.4 cm)

Outer Border
Cut 5 1/2″ (14 cm) wide

Instructions

Sew each sky triangle to a dark triangle to make 2 two-colored blocks. Appliqué leaves on the individual blocks. On the two-colored blocks, the diagonal seams must be covered with leaves or flowers. Remember that a few of the leaves will be appliquéd after the border is attached. Appliqué florets: Start at the outer edges of desired floral shape (no more than 7″ [17.8 cm] in diameter) and overlap the florets to create clusters of blooms. Work toward the center of each cluster.

Attach the narrow borders to each block. Using diagram 1 as a guide, lay out the blocks so you know where to attach the sashing pieces. Sew the short sashing strips to the required blocks. Sew the blocks in rows and sew the rows to the long sashing strips. Attach the border and miter the corners. Appliqué the final leaves, which extend through the window structure.

Quilting

Quilt around flowers, around leaves, and leaf veins. Random quilt sky to resemble clouds.

Diagram 1

Autumn: Pride Goeth Before the Fall
Kathleen M. O'Hanlon
59″ x 42″ (150 cm x 107 cm)
Machine pieced, appliquéd, and quilted

Autumn: Pride Goeth Before the Fall

When I am creating quilt art, I am suspended in a timeless place, totally absorbed by the moment. I have found it empowering to grow in my affirmation as a quilt artist over time and discover my creativity and the path it will take me on.

An idea has to percolate for a long time before I feel ready to begin a quilt. The fabric is the fun part of creating art, starting with color. I love watching how the first fabrics I choose are simple or basic, predictable, but then I pull in several other colors until there's a much richer palette. I spend a lot of time looking at various fabrics together before anything takes shape. I would love to be the kind of person that intuitively throws swatches up on the wall that work first try. But the actual work with the fabric, the color and the creation of art, is the most important to me.

My inspiration from nature does not come from actual scenes. Often, it's the juxtaposition of color that I see in person or in a photograph that inspires me. In nature, the beauty is in color. I don't need a complete vision in my head to have a quilt evolve; in fact, I prefer not to. I'm not bound to the first image of my quilt at all, and I trust the process. I don't look at each piece as a challenge. For me, it's the excitement of creating. I want people to be drawn into my art, not detached, but involved.

Kathleen M. O'Hanlon

INSPIRATION

For Kathleen, autumn is actually two seasons, beginning when the trees are covered with leaves in rich, vibrant colors and culminating when the leaves drop off, leaving the trees bare. She wanted her quilt to reflect both of these images, and because she is fascinated by the beauty of diagonal Japanese quilts, she wanted her quilt to also have a Japanese influence.

Kathleen studied leaves and how the sky affects their color, incorporating into her quilt fall colored leaves and changeable skies of gray and blue, sprinkled with floating white clouds. The wind carelessly lifts and twirls the leaves about.

This design actually came to Kathleen during an improvisational dance class, where she danced the graceful movements of the wind, felt the crisp coolness of the fall air, and imagined the fall leaves swirling about her.

TECHNIQUE

Fabric Requirements

Central Medallion and Outer Pieced Border
1½ yards (137 cm) assorted scraps in autumn colors

Yellow Border
⅜ yard (34 cm)

Second Border
⅜ yard (34 cm) each of three autumn colors

Rust Border
¾ yard (69 cm)

Black Framing and Binding
⅝ yard (57 cm)

Hanging Loops
(Optional) ½ yard (46 cm)

Cutting

Central Medallion
Cut 52—Template A
Cut 52—Template B
Cut 46—Template C
Cut 14—Template D
Cut 3—Template E
Cut 3—Template F

Note: Cut extras so you can substitute pleasing fabrics and placements once you begin to work on your design wall.

Yellow Border
Cut 4—2¼″ x 42″ (5.7 cm x 107 cm)

Second Border
Cut 2—4½″ x 42″ (11.4 cm x 107 cm) of three different fabrics

Black Framing
Cut 6—1″ x 42″ (2.5 cm x 107 cm)

Rust Border
Cut 2—2½″ x 42" (6.4 cm x 107 cm)
Cut 2— 9″ x 42″ (22.9 cm x 107 cm)

Outer Pieced Border
Cut approximately 70 rectangles 2¼″ (5.7 cm) wide, in a variety of lengths ranging from 1¼″ (3.2 cm) to 2½″ (6.4 cm)

Binding
Cut 6—2″ x 42″ (5.1 cm x 107 cm)

Hanging Loops
Cut 3—4½″ x 42″ (11.4 cm x 107 cm)

Assembly

The central medallion is composed of forty-nine 4″ (10.2 cm) finished square units. Each of these units is pieced from various combinations of Templates A through F. See diagram 1 for suggested piecing of these units. Compose a pleasing arrangement of 7 x 7 units, using Templates A through F for each unit. When you are happy with the arrangement, sew the units. Each unit will measure 4½″ (11.4 cm) square unfinished. Sew the 7 rows of 7 units together to complete the central medallion.

Sew a yellow border strip to the top and bottom of the central medallion, then sew a yellow border strip to each side.

Decide how each of the three chosen fabrics will wrap around the second border. Use diagrams 2 and 3 as guides for sewing the strips of fabric together at 45 degree angles. Sew the unpieced strip of fabric to the top of the quilt. Sew the joined strip of fabrics 2 and 3 to the bottom of the quilt, positioning the 45 degree seam as desired. Position the final joined strip where desired on the right side of the quilt. Attach the strip and cut off the excess. Position and sew the excess strip to the left side of the quilt.

Sew a black framing strip to the top and bottom of the

quilt, then sew a black framing strip to each side. Sew a 2 ½″ (6.4 cm) rust border strip to the top and bottom of the quilt. Attach a 9″ (22.9 cm) rust border strip to each side. Sew a black framing strip to the right and left sides of the rust border. Sew assorted rectangles randomly together for the outer pieced border, creating two strips each 2¼″ (5.7 cm) by approximately 42″ (107 cm). Sew a strip to both sides of the quilt.

Appliqué one triangle using Template A and four triangles using Template B to the quilt using the photo as a guide for placement.

Quilting

Quilt as desired. Bind with black binding.

To create six hanging loops for the quilt, fold black strips in half lengthwise, right sides together, and stitch the length of the strips. Turn. Measure to desired length for hanging from stick, adding ½″ (13 mm). Cut. Stitch across the ends of each length to create six loops. Hand sew loops to top back of quilt.

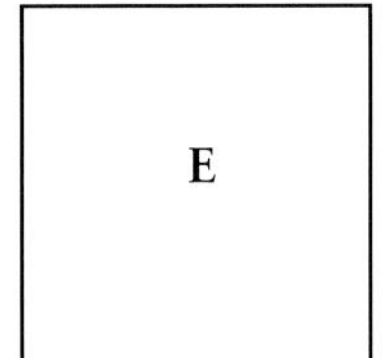

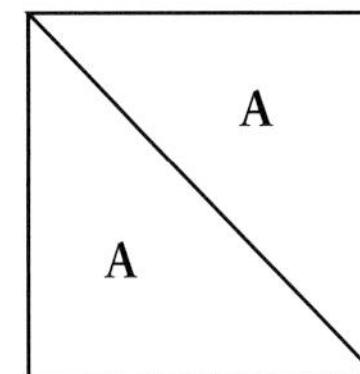

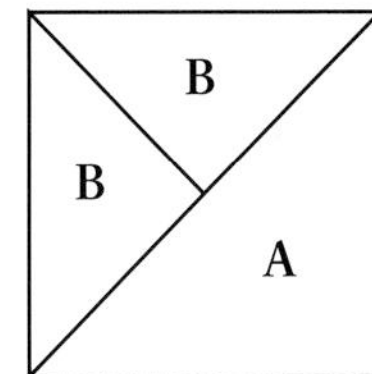

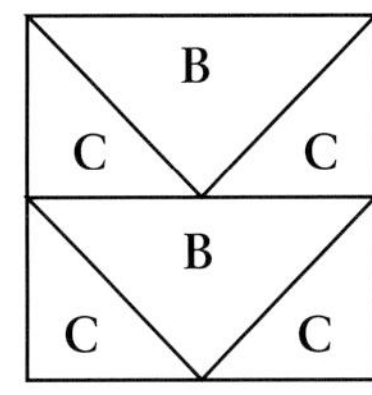

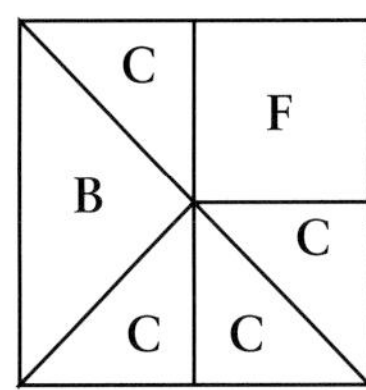

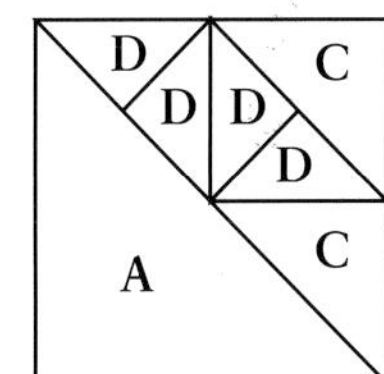

Diagram 1

Diagram 2

Diagram 3

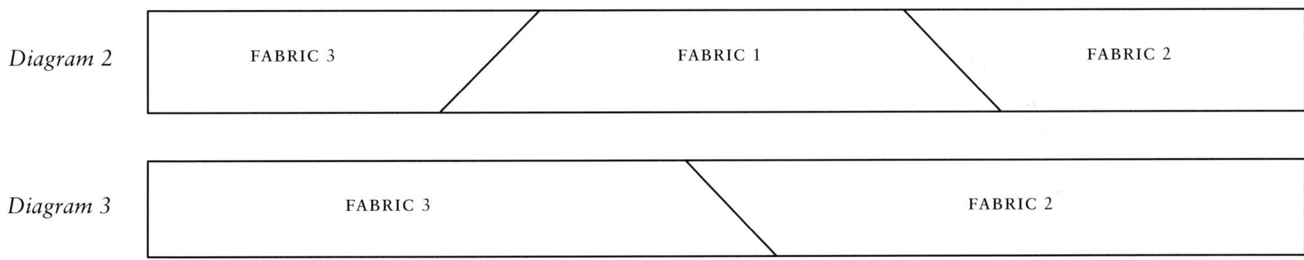

Diagram 4

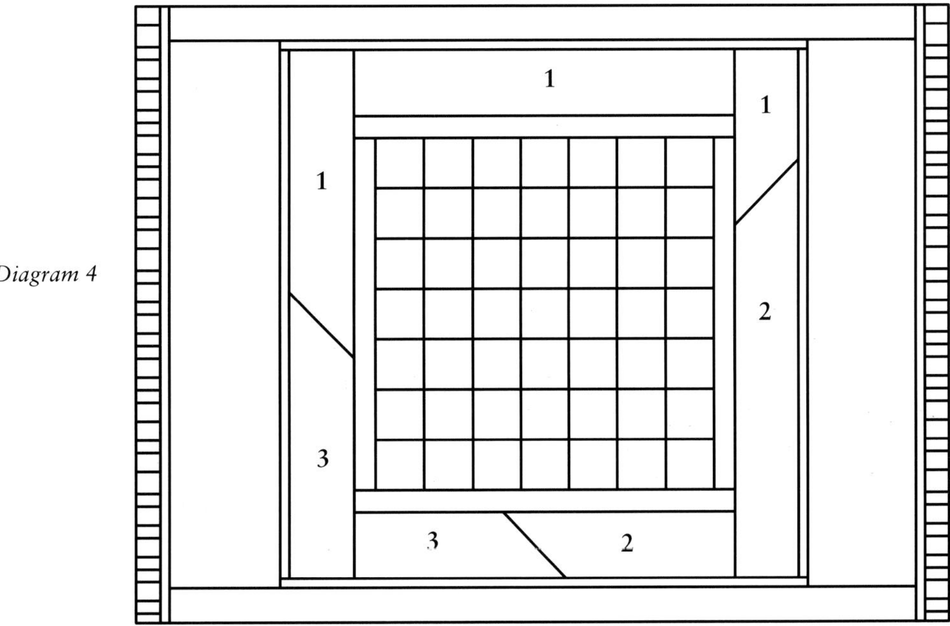

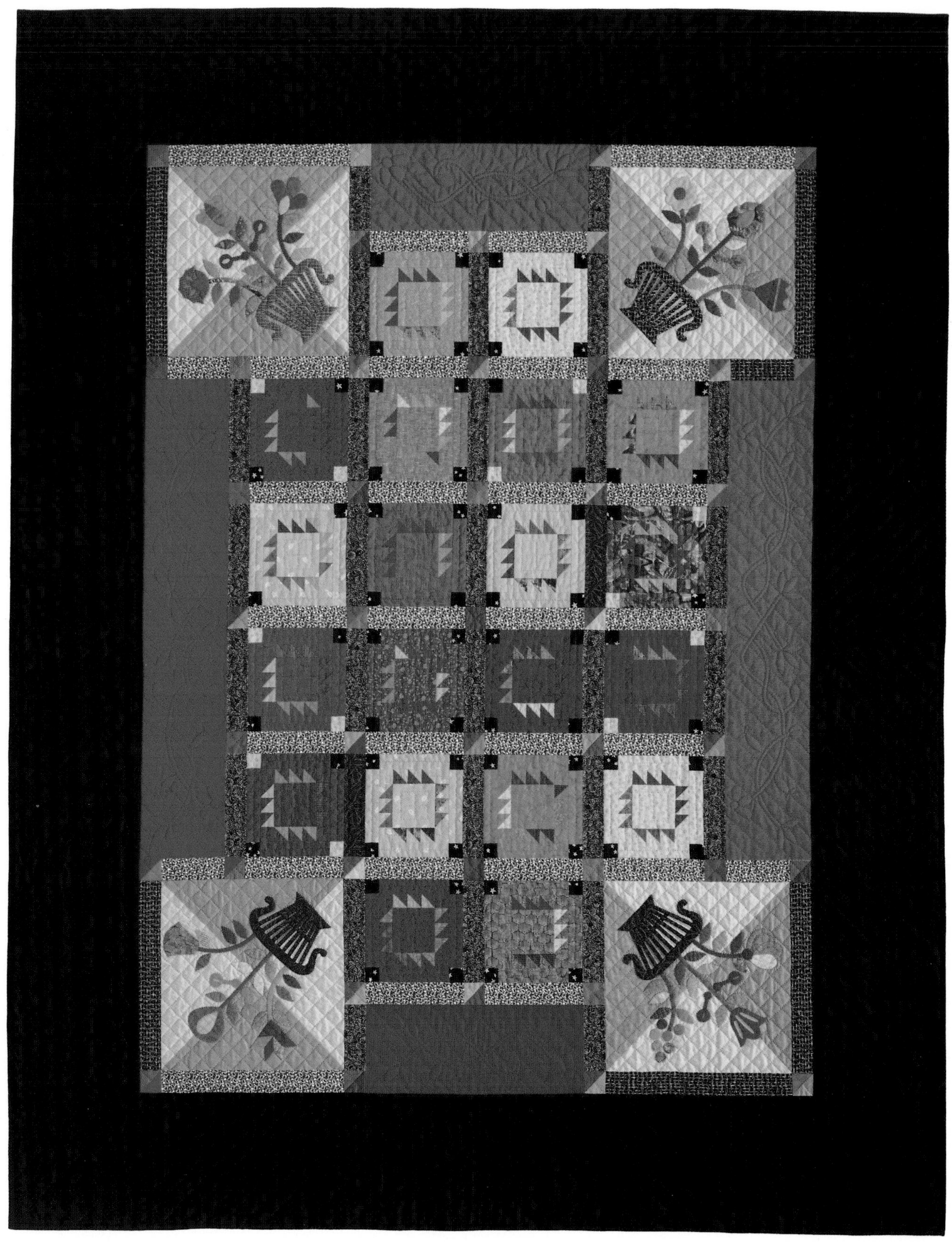

Nightshades
Heather W. Tewell
Collection of Mae Waldron; 64″ x 82″ (165 cm x 208 cm)
Machine pieced, hand appliquéd and quilted, color and value interplay

Nightshades

I DON'T WANT people to say my quilts are beautiful, I want them to see that each quilt works as a unified whole, with push and pull and some tug to it. I like the complexity of quilting and the possibilities. There's a line you cross when your work becomes art. I believe each person has to build a store of knowledge before he or she can create art. Each quilt I make is a challenge and it solves a problem. When I challenge myself, I stretch myself to use alternative mediums and techniques. I like fitting the fabric to the design, choosing fabric that enhances the design element, making it work. I want my work to be artistic, unique, free, and less rooted in tradition, and I live for the actual process of making quilts and crave the doing of it.

My quilts stay in my imagination all of the time. It seems as though often, unconsciously, I will begin thinking about a quilt as I go thorough my day, and solutions for a particular problem related to the quilt will pop out of nowhere.

Quilting fills all of the spaces in my house and my brain. I see colors when I travel, and I constantly watch and scheme for ideas for quilts. When I am out in nature, I remain open to seeing things I've never seen before. I'm always plotting about my sources for my quilts, and I don't worry about the dry periods. I know that after the drought, there will be a flood of ideas.

Heather W Tewell

INSPIRATION

The inspiration for Nightshades is multileveled. According to Heather, Nightshades is meant to "show the mysterious, sinister shades of the night sky in the Northwest, yet also the beauty of it," with the secondary theme depicting the deadly nightshade weed that grows abundantly throughout the Northwest. Heather specifically used intense colors in her work that look like "animals' eyes that glow in the dark night sky." The color purple signifies both the bloom of the deadly nightshade weed, and the illusion of a ghost who comes out only at night.

The sashing between the star blocks use varied black prints, demonstrating Heather's philosophy that as long as the value reads constant, it doesn't matter what fabric you choose.

For the four corners of her quilt, Heather used a basket block by Elly Sienkiewicz, incorporating her own flowers and leaves into the design.

TECHNIQUE

7″ x 7″ (17.8 cm x 17.8 cm) pieced blocks
13″ x 13″ (33 cm x 33 cm) appliquéd blocks

Fabric Requirements

PIECED BLOCKS
1½ yards (137 cm) assorted fuchsias
1½ yards (137 cm) assorted golds

APPLIQUÉD BLOCKS
½ yard (57 cm) light, ½ yard (57 cm) dark

ASSORTED SCRAPS FOR BASKET APPLIQUÉ

SASHING
1 yard (91 cm) assorted blacks

INNER BORDER
1 yard (91 cm) assorted hot pinks

OUTER BORDER
2 yards (183 cm) black

Cutting

PIECED BLOCKS
Cut for 20 blocks, using Templates A, B, C, and D

APPLIQUÉD BLOCKS
Cut 2 light and 2 dark 14½″ (36.8 cm) squares; cut diagonally twice

SASHING
Cut 43 light and 43 dark triangles, using Template E
Cut 50—2″ x 7½″ (5.1 cm x 19.1 cm)
Cut 8—2″ x 5″ (5.1 cm x 12.7 cm)
Cut 8—2″ x 13½″ (5.1 cm x 34.3 cm)

BORDERS
Cut 2—6½″ x 16″ (16.5 cm x 40.6 cm) inner border
Cut 2—6½″ x 33″ (16.5 cm x 83.8 cm) inner border
Cut 2—9½″ x 66″ (16.5 cm x 167.6 cm) side outer borders
Cut 2—9½″ x 65″ (16.5 cm x 165.1 cm) top and bottom outer border

Assembly

Construct 20 pieced blocks following diagram 1. Blocks measure 7½″ (19.1 cm) unfinished. Piece 4 corner blocks for appliqué. See diagram 2. Select a basket block of your choice and enlarge or reduce it to fit the corner blocks. Use your favorite method of appliqué. Sew 43 half square triangles for pieced sashing. Use diagram 3 as a guide for assembling blocks, sashing, and inner borders. You may stuff the inner borders if you wish. Select a design that enhances the quilt and fits into the space.

Sew outer borders to the sides of the quilt, then attach top and bottom borders to complete the quilt top.

Quilting

Use your favorite method of quilting to finish the quilt.

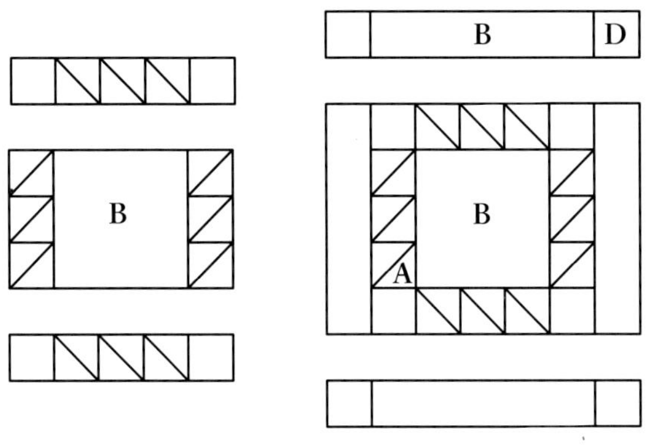

Diagram 1

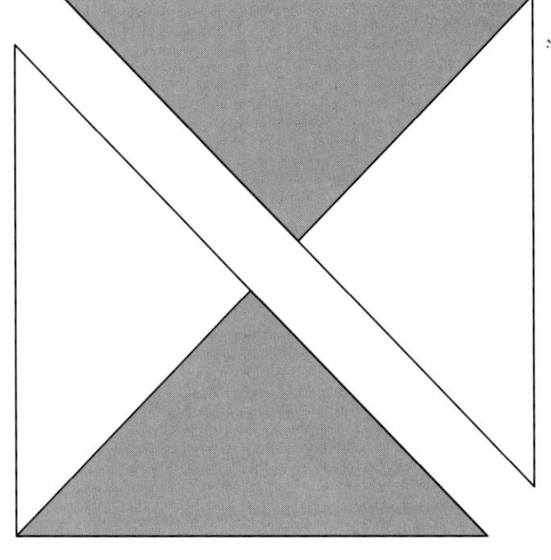
Diagram 2

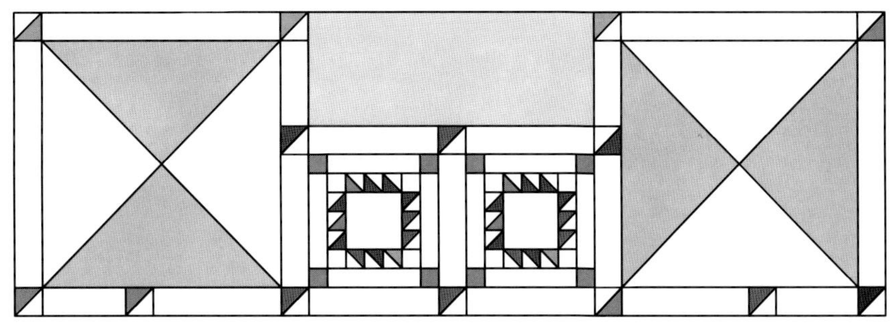

Diagram 3

Palouse Puzzle
Karen Schoepflin Hagen
82″ x 105″ (208 cm x 267 cm)
Needle-turn appliquéd, hand quilted

Palouse Puzzle

I FEEL LUCKY to have found what I am meant to do in my life. The passion I possess for my quilting comes from wanting to share my quilts with someone else. I wish I had the time to execute all of the ideas in my head.

Nature really touches and calls out to me, and many of my quilts are nature inspired. Some of my quilts come from words as well as ideas. The ideas for my quilts always come first. I have already sketched enough to take three or four lifetimes to complete. I don't use graph paper for my appliqué quilts. I like to cut my fabric free hand into the shapes I need. When I select my fabrics, I just pull out all the colors I need. I try and use numerous prints together to get what I call an "eye mix" when I am making ground cover. A quilt can be made fifty different ways, and I try not to agonize over the color decisions; I go with my first impulse when selecting the fabrics and colors.

When my quilt is cut out, I lay everything on the floor and pin it down. I use needle turn appliqué for most of my designs, coupled with a pieced border. I love laying out the quilt and the hand appliqué. When I do the hand quilting, it's like I am taking a nap, the enjoyment is so strong. It's a time I enjoy and it is the crowning end to my art.

Karen Schoepflin Hagen

INSPIRATION

This quilt captures the flavor of the wheat fields, rolling hills, and Moscow Mountain, near Karen's home in the Palouse region of Idaho. She designed this quilt as a tribute to her father, Howard Schoepflin. Growing up on a dairy and wheat farm, she remembers her dad out in a combine, harvesting wheat and grain crops.

Karen came up with the name Palouse Puzzle before she began the work and challenged herself to create the piece like it was a giant puzzle. It was intentionally left without borders because a puzzle almost never has a frame. This theme makes her quilt intriguing and full of options. Karen's final touch was to hand quilt 1,200 jigsaw-puzzle piece shapes over the entire quilt.

What do you see around you in nature that would translate into a quilt with a puzzle format?

CHAPTER 2 *Dawn to Dusk*

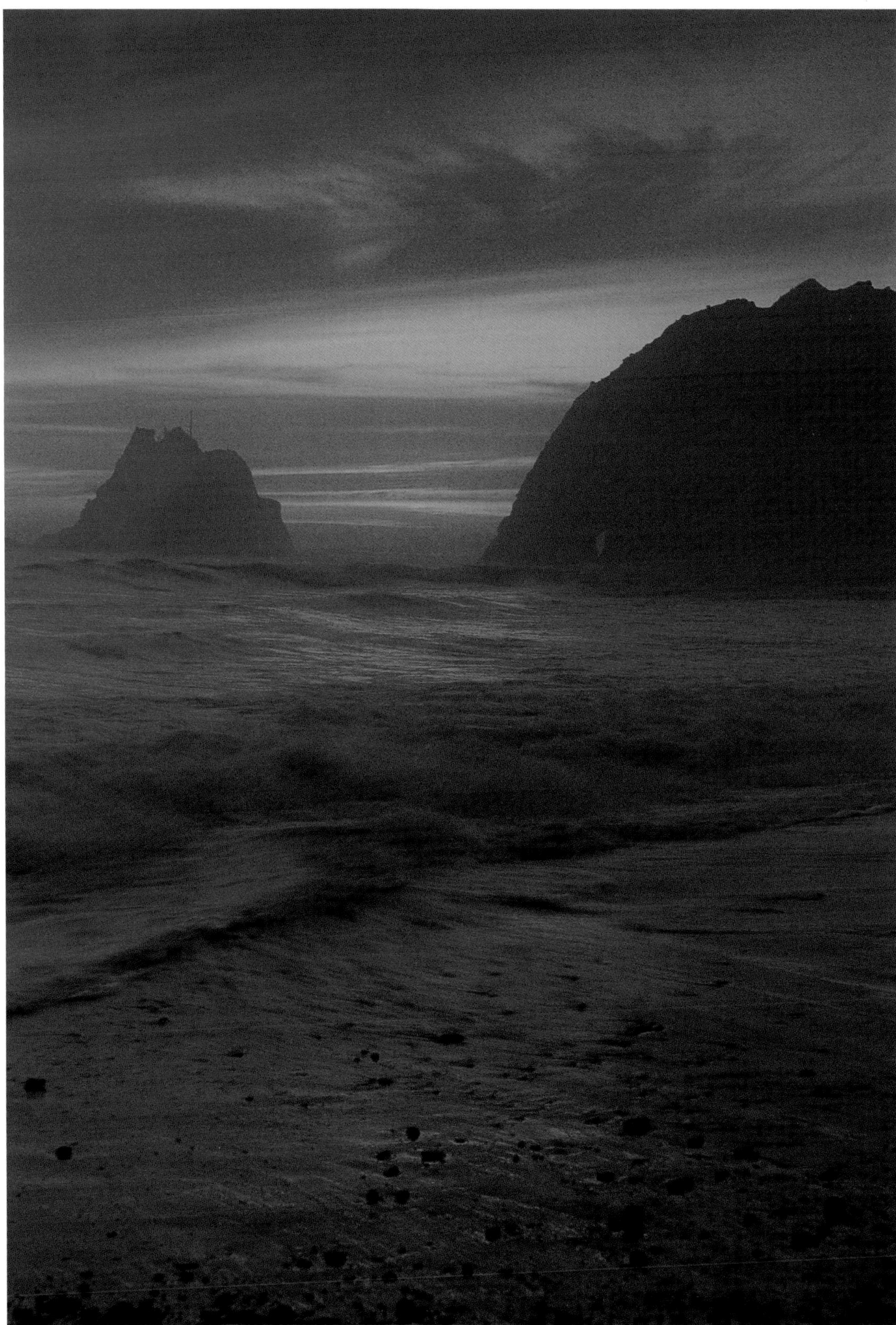

Red sunset at Hole-in-the Wall headland, Olympic National Park, WA.

Denali Lights
Ree Nancarrow
Assembled by members of Cabin Fever Quilter's Guild, Fairbanks, Alaska
Quilted by Gail Flodin
Collection of Cabin Fever Quilter's Guild
78″ x 52″ (198 cm x 132 cm)
String paper piecing, machine quilted

Denali Lights

I THINK QUILT MAKING is growing unlike any other art form. We are on the edge of producing new and unusual ways of expressing ourselves in our quilt art. We owe a great deal to the artists that have gone before us and paved the way by setting up a structure for us, presenting quilt shows and exhibitions that legitimize quilt making.

Although I come from an art background and have been involved with art all of my life, I find that with quilt making, I can express myself with fabric, creating a unique look and aura that fits what I am trying to say. My art is so interactive, it just evolves. I am continually thinking ahead, "Gosh, what would happen if I did this or that"; it's definitely an evolving process. It's wonderful to be able to make a technique do whatever you need it to do so that you can carry out your idea for a particular quilt.

The whole process of quilt making is exciting to me. I flex as I go, making changes and rethinking each quilt all the way to its end. Color is important to me because it expresses the feel of the idea I am trying to convey.

I am passionate about my quilt making. Once I get going, there's no stopping me. But if a project isn't a challenge, I don't even bother with it. If I find a technically difficult project, I work with ideas until I find a way to complete it. My ideas are triggered by life around me, and I particularly enjoy combining the close up and far away parts of nature in my nature quilts.

Ree Nancarrow

INSPIRATION

Ree designed this quilt made by a group of women from the Cabin Fever Quilter's Guild for permanent loan to the Denali Center, a long-term health care facility in Fairbanks, Alaska. The following women helped piece and bind this quilt: Trish DeLong, Kathy Dubbs, Martie Hall, Gayle Hazen, Lucy McCarthy, Norma Mosso, Nancy Norum, Shirley Phelps, Julie Scott, and Ingrid Taylor. Gail Flodin quilted the work.

Ree lives in Denali Park, 135 miles from Fairbanks, so it was not easy for her to participate in the actual sewing of the design. When she designed the quilt, Ree says, "It was important for me to come up with something the residents of the Denali Center would enjoy living with, and since the Northern Lights are typically Alaskan, I felt the senior citizens would enjoy this theme." Ree also wanted to stretch the technical limits of the women constructing the quilt, but knew her instructions needed to be "clear and concise enough that they could execute it without me."

Ree wanted to "convey ribbons of color" through an abstract design rather than through a realistic approach. For those of us not fortunate enough to have witnessed the Northern Lights in person, Ree describes them as "really bright, and when there is a colorful night, they ripple across the sky, with the brighter colors near the top, with tones fading out toward the horizon."

TECHNIQUE

Fabric Suggestions and Requirements

Select solid fabrics in color ranges of greens, yellows, oranges, and reds for the bands of Northern Lights. Select four dark blue print fabrics that grade nicely in value from almost black to medium blue for the sky; and blue print fabrics that grade in value from light blue to medium blue for the mountains.

1/4 yard (23 cm) each of at least 15 yellows, oranges, and reds
1/4 yard (23 cm) each of at least 15 yellows and greens
1 1/4 yards (114 cm) each of four blue sky fabrics
1/4 yard (23 cm) each of at least 8 light to medium blues for mountains

Cutting

Cut solid fabrics in assorted strips from 3/4″ (1.9 cm) to 2 1/4″ (5.7 cm) wide
Cut mountain fabrics in assorted strips from 1″ (2.5 cm) to 2″ (5.1 cm) wide
Cut sky fabrics using enlarged templates

Instructions

Using an opaque projector, enlarge each panel in diagram 1 to full size and draw it on white butcher paper. Letter and number all pieces and cut them apart. Cut the sky pieces from the blue print fabrics. Use sections A, C, E, and G as template patterns, adding 1/4″ (6 mm) seam allowance. String piece the Northern Light sections using assorted widths of solid color fabrics for use in sections B, D, and F, going from light to dark, as required. Use the yellow through red strips for the B section, and the yellow through green strips for the D section. Use leftovers from the B and D sections for the F strips, but use only the lighter colors. Add 1/4″ (6 mm) seam allowances to the template pieces. String piece the mountain section using the light to medium blue fabrics. Use the H sections as templates. Sew each mountain H piece to the sky G piece above it, then sew each Ga/Ha unit to each Gb/Hb unit. Sew all of the 1 sections together; repeat for each section. Using your design wall, find the most pleasing arrangement. Sew all sections together.

Quilting

Quilt using your favorite method.

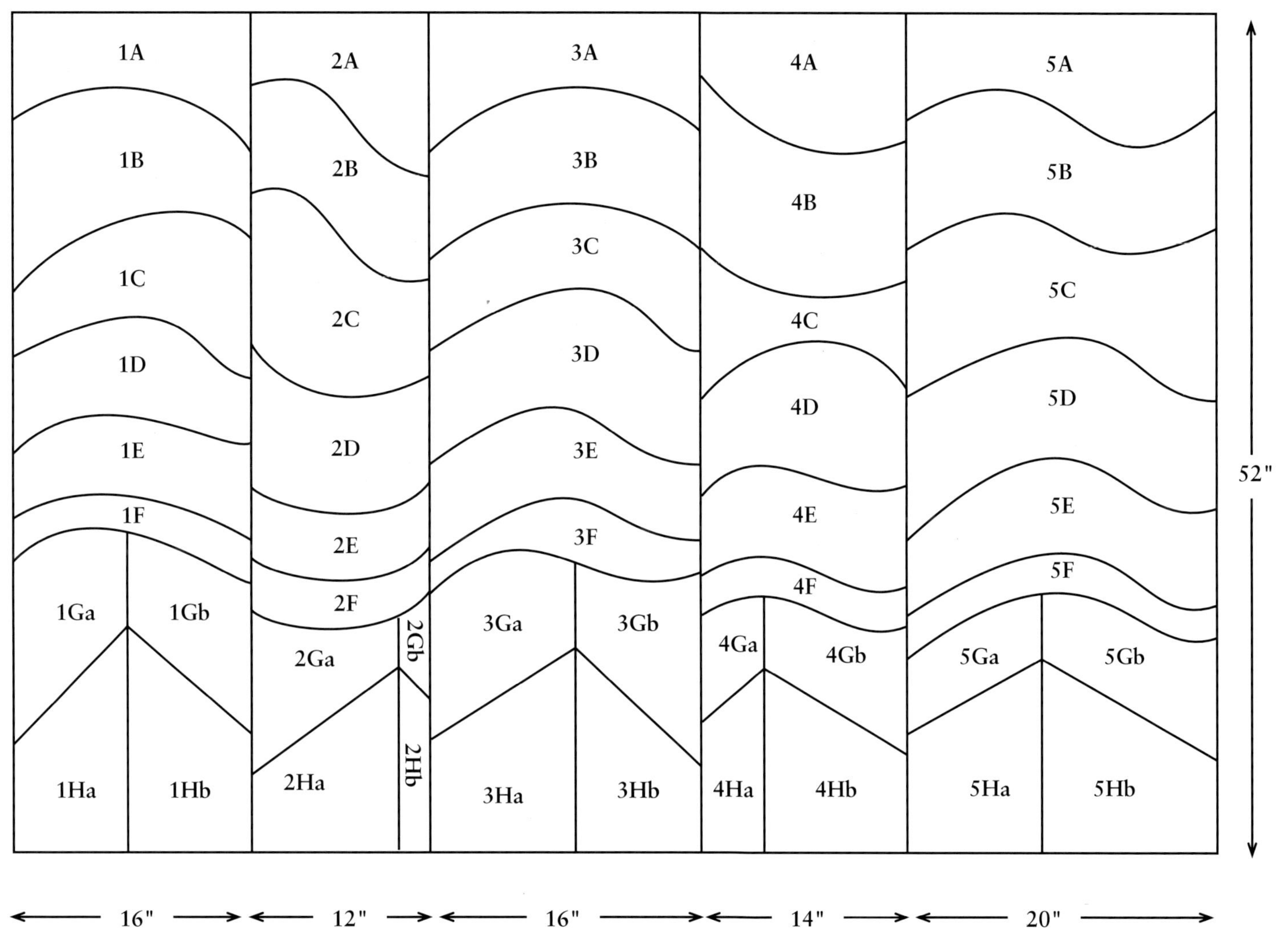
1A
1B
1C
1D
1E
1F
1Ga
1Gb
1Ha
1Hb
2A
2B
2C
2D
2E
2F
2Ga
2Gb
2Ha
2Hb
3A
3B
3C
3D
3E
3F
3Ga
3Gb
3Ha
3Hb
4A
4B
4C
4D
4E
4F
4Ga
4Gb
4Ha
4Hb
5A
5B
5C
5D
5E
5F
5Ga
5Gb
5Ha
5Hb
52"
16"
12"
16"
14"
20"

Diagram 1

Starry Starry Night
Deborah White
Wall Quilt 64″ x 64″ (163 cm x 163 cm)
Miniature Quilt 16″ x 16″ (41 cm x 41 cm)
Machine pieced, hand quilted, Ohio Star variation

Starry Starry Night

I CAN'T HELP but receive inspiration from nature and include it in my art; it's all around me. I am fascinated with flowers and stars. When I'm designing a quilt inspired by nature, the color choices come first, then I'll adapt the design to the color.

I have always had the need to create things. I feel it is a God-given need. Once I figured out that's why I have the drive to create things, it all clicked together in my quilting.

To me, the designing and color selection in quilt making are the most important factors. I've always been intrigued by working with color combinations for impact in my work. Generally, I have my color pallets in mind for a quilt before I start pulling fabrics. My emotions are often reflected by the color choices I make as I design a quilt. I feel color, I don't just use it.

I have always been a perfectionist, so the technical part of quilt making is automatic. The frustrating part is when I see a picture in my mind that I can't quite reproduce. Only now do I feel I am heading in the right direction because I am willing to take chances in my quilting.

I'm a fanatic when it comes to quilt making. I never stop. I have ideas popping up in my head constantly. My brain is always thinking quilts. It's a driving energy that I can't squelch. My quilting keeps me sane and keeps my mind balanced. My quilts are the delight of my day, something to look forward to.

Deborah White

INSPIRATION

Debbie's inspiration for this quilt came while star gazing in her backyard. When she and her daughter, Cheri, used to look at the stars together, Cheri would always say, "Stars, lots and lots of stars." Debbie wanted to create a quilt that reflected the poignancy of those moments. When contemplating a night sky, Debbie says she thinks of it as "multicolored with sparkling stars and planets," rather than as planets and stars that are stark white.

Debbie is fortunate to live on the Kitsap Peninsula near the waters of Puget Sound where nature's inspiration is abundant. She very rarely uses a published pattern for her miniature quilts and more often than not, her inspiration for a quilt is sparked by an idea or emotion. For her border, Debbie used Sally Schneider's *Painless Borders* technique. Her original quilt is made in miniature, but she has furnished directions for a nine-inch block.

TECHNIQUE

9˝ x 9˝ (22.9 cm x 22.9 cm) blocks for wall quilt
2¼˝ x 2¼˝ (5.7 cm x 5.7 cm) blocks for miniature quilt

Fabric Suggestions

If you are making this into a miniature, shop for fabrics with a small scale print. Large prints get lost or take up the entire design when used in miniatures. If you are making this into a wall quilt, your scale can be larger, but the scale must still be subdued, not dominant.

Fabric Requirements (Wall Quilt)

½ yard (46 cm) each of several fuchsia prints, light to dark
½ yard (46 cm) each of several blue prints, light to dark
1 yard (91 cm) mustard print
2 yards (183 cm) black print

Fabric Requirements (Miniature Quilt)

¼ yard (23 cm) each of several fuchsia prints, light to dark
¼ yard (23 cm) each of several blue prints, light to dark
½ yard (46 cm) mustard print
1 yard (91 cm) black print

Instructions

WALL QUILT

Block 1 Make 9 using Templates A and B
Block 2 Make 4 using Templates A, C, D, E, and F
Block 3 Make 8 using Templates C and G
Block 4 Make 4 using Templates C and G
Block 5 Make 8 using Templates A, C, and H
Block 6 Make 4 using Templates A, C, and H
Block 7 Make 4 using Templates A, C, and H

For Template F, cut rectangle 3½˝ x 9½˝ (8.9 cm x 24.1 cm)
For Template G, cut square 9½˝ (25.1 cm)

SIDE TRIANGLES

Make 16 Cut 4—14˝ (35.6 cm) squares. Cut each square diagonally twice.

CORNER TRIANGLES

Make 4 Cut 2—9⅞˝ (25.1 cm) squares. Cut each square diagonally once.

Assembly

Make all the necessary blocks. If you have questions regarding block assembly, refer to *Painless Borders* listed in Resources. As an alternative, Debbie suggests using this resource for half-square and quarter-square triangles. Sew the blocks in rows, adding the side and corner triangles as shown in the assembly diagram.

Quilting

Quilt using your favorite method.

MINIATURE QUILT

To make a miniature quilt, use the actual size drawings to make templates, add seam allowances, and follow the assembly instructions above.

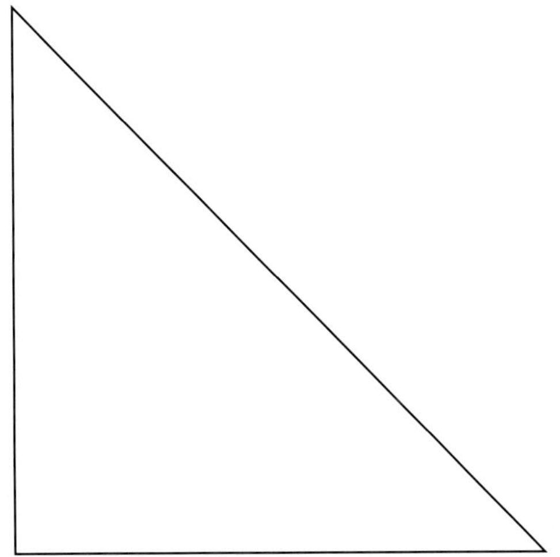

Side Triangle
MAKE 16

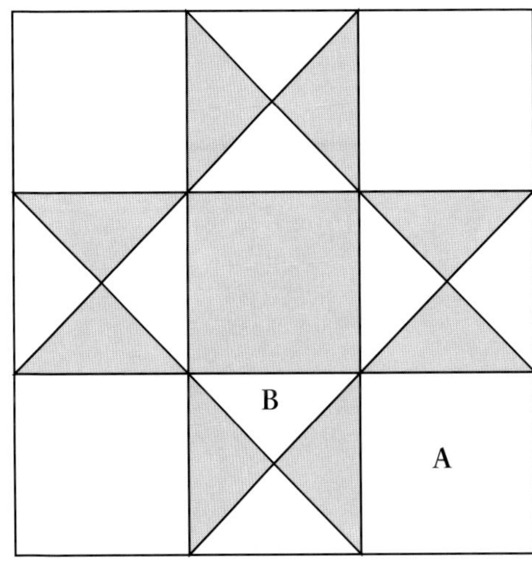

Block 1
MAKE 9

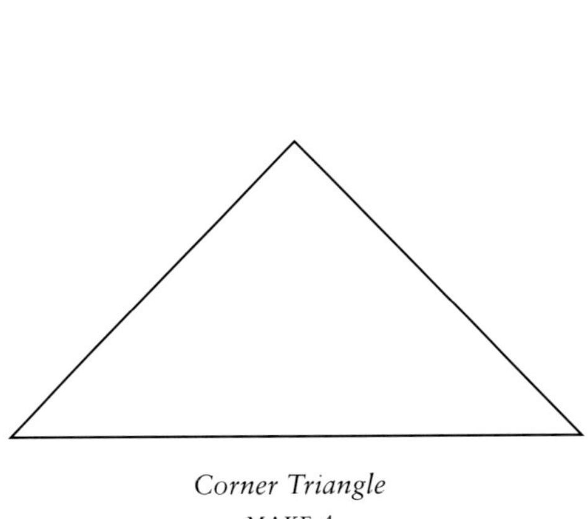

Corner Triangle
MAKE 4

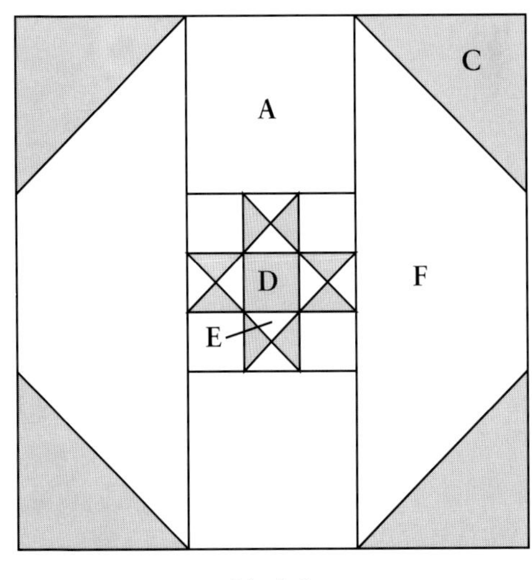

Block 2
MAKE 4

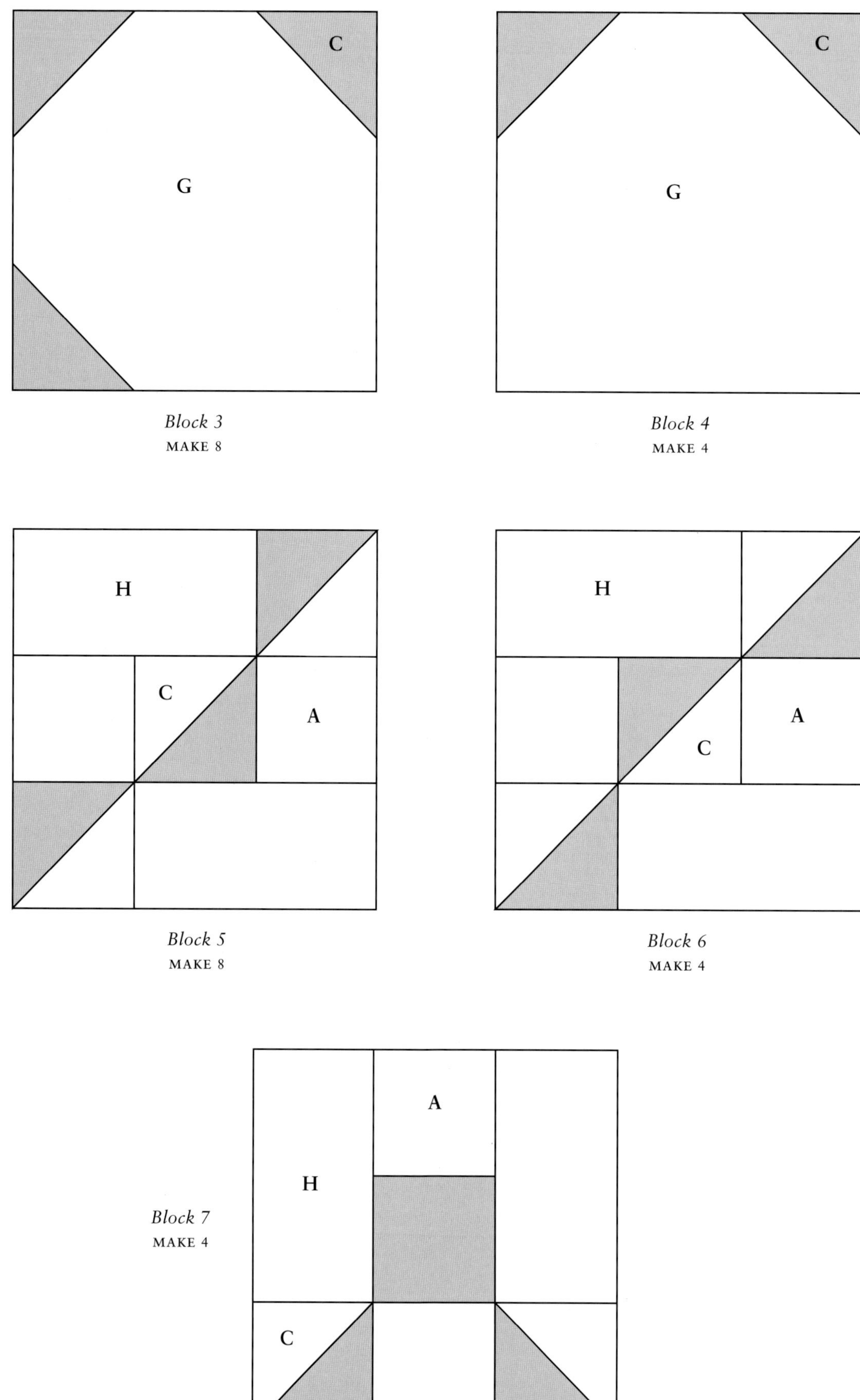

Block 3
MAKE 8

Block 4
MAKE 4

Block 5
MAKE 8

Block 6
MAKE 4

Block 7
MAKE 4

Assembly Diagram

Orion Rising
Melody Crust
62″ x 84″ (157 cm x 213 cm)
Machine pieced and quilted, beaded

Orion Rising

I LIKE EVERYTHING that quilting offers me—the people, the color, the fabric, and the teaching. I am passionate about quilting and it's very much a part of my life. Quilting is always in my mind and it's usually not very subconscious. I like the tactile properties of fabric, the process of making a quilt, and I love the agony of making all the decisions.

I probably get the most inspiration from flowers for my nature quilts; I make a lot of quilts where the underlying theme is flowers. My husband and I travel a lot so nature is always with me and I can't divorce myself from what I see, the color combinations, for example.

I cannot begin designing a quilt until I picture it in my mind, but I understand that what I see in my head and the finished piece will not necessarily be the same. Typically, I put some ideas down on paper. I call them road maps to start from, just sketches. Then, I put tracing paper over my sketch and color it. I may use several tracings with different colors so I'll get the color idea I like. Then I start playing with fabric. When I pull fabrics, I usually have enough on hand, supplementing it if I need to with purchased fabric. If my idea doesn't work on my design wall, I'll play with it until it does.

Each piece of my art is a challenge. Generally, I try something I haven't done before because I'm not interested in making the same quilt more than once.

Melody Crust

INSPIRATION

The inspiration for Orion Rising occurred when Melody was traveling on a photo shoot with her husband, Charles. It was dawn, and as Melody says, "The sky had that predawn richness." She was fascinated by the way the sky lightened and wanted to capture this effect in her quilt. The sunrise is demonstrated by the reddish glow at the bottom of the quilt, gradually changing to blues. Melody agonized over locating a book that would give her "a map of the sky," while all the while, Charles had the perfect one tucked away.

Orion Rising is the star with a reddish cast, and the Milky Way is the heavily beaded area that flows through the whole quilt. Melody uses a wide variety of quilting thread in her machine quilting and says she probably spends as much on thread as she does on fabric. She feels quilting thread offers design qualities that many quilters overlook and suggests large sewing machine stores as a resource.

TECHNIQUE

Fabric Suggestions

Choose a variety of prints from light to dark values in hues of deep red to pink and dark blue to light blue. Pieced stars are done in shades of yellow to gold, blues, and reds.

Instructions

This design is based on two-inch units composed of squares and half-square triangles. The Star blocks are combinations of these units. Star blocks are 6″ (15.2 cm) and 8″ (20.3 cm) square. The LeMoyne Star is 12" (30.5 cm) square, and the elongated Ohio Star is a 12″ x 16″ (30.5 cm x 40.6 cm) block. The fabric manipulation adds to the appearance of a larger variety of blocks.

Cut 2½″ (6.4 cm) squares in a variety of colors and fabrics to begin the design process. Use your favorite method of piecing half-square triangles or refer to *Quilts! Quilts!! Quilts!!!*

Assembly

To assemble the 6″ (15.2 cm) and 8″ (20.3 cm) star blocks, sew the rows together as in diagram 1. The 12″ x 16″ (30.5 cm x 40.6 cm) Ohio Star block is assembled in the order shown in diagram 2. The 12″ (30.5 cm) Lemoyne Star blocks are pieced by joining the G units together and insetting the H and I pieces in the traditional method as in diagram 3. Consider selective cutting of Template G. Assemble the quilt in sections and rows using the diagram as a guide.

Quilting

The quilting design is the Milky Way surrounded by masses of swirling gases. Use a large variety of metallic threads for the machine quilting. The Milky Way is defined with heavy beading.

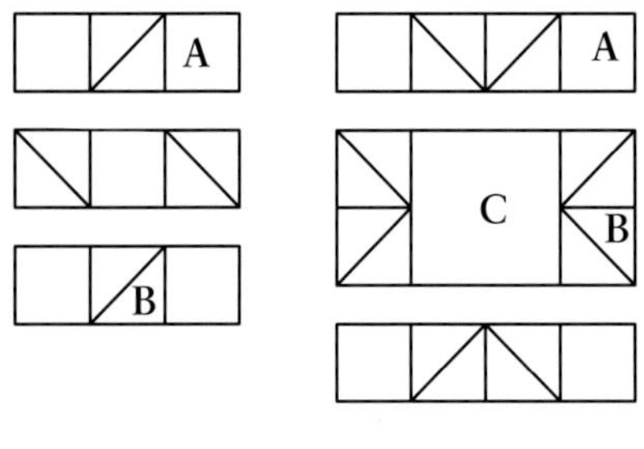

Diagram 1

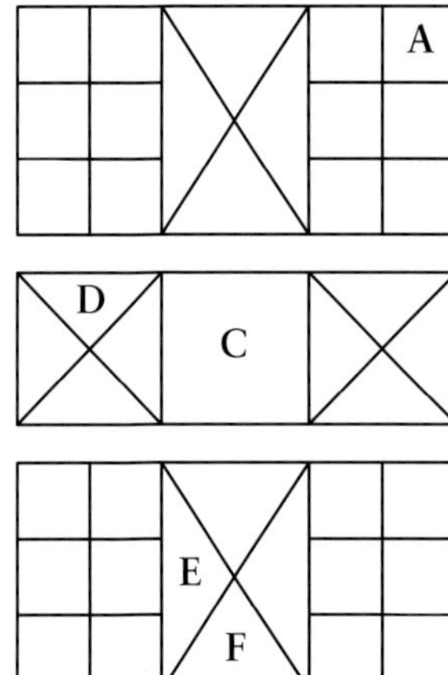

Diagram 2

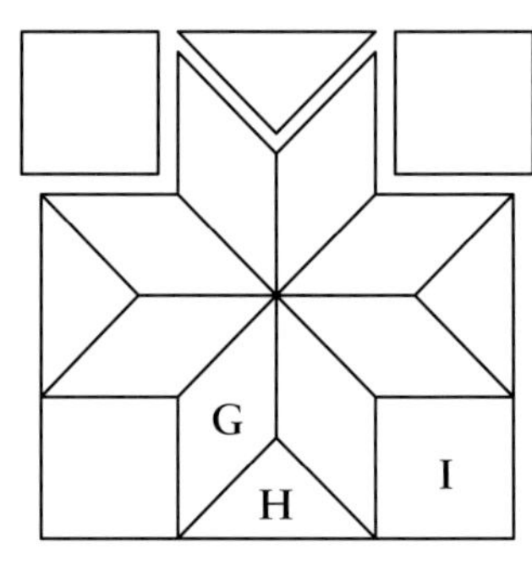

Diagram 3

Assembly Diagram

Village Sunrise
Barbara Lee Olson
47″ x 41″ (119 cm x 104 cm) without borders
Machine pieced, appliquéd, and quilted, designing with light and illusion

Village Sunrise

I HAVE A DEFINITE FEELING that I am doing what I was meant to do with my life. I feel I can affect people with the energy I present in my quilt art by sharing my works, hoping they evoke hope and joy.

I'm a visual person, and when I discovered quilting, I felt like I had come home. Usually, I start with a broad concept or even a minute idea for my quilts and put something on my design wall. I use a picture or shape that has inspired me as a beginning point, and then I let the quilt evolve. It's like I am in control to a certain point, and then I have to let the quilt take on a life of its own. Even though I have a mental image, I feel a stronger force works through me to create my quilts.

I am not a purist, and I have no problem using glue, paper, or any medium to get my designs applied to the fabric. With each piece of art, I advance and get braver. For me, being free enough to take these risks allows me to create art quilts.

I enjoy seeing how light plays on different forms in nature and incorporating these images into my art. Quilting is an art form unlike any other. I find it much more intriguing than painting because you can create so much texture and depth. Part of my mission is to educate those around me that quilting is not a craft, but art. I want people to feel the energy in my quilts, to experience the emotion and be mesmerized.

Barbara Olson

INSPIRATION

Barbara is married to a Native American and lives close to the Crow Reservation in Idaho. She "wanted to create the feel and emotion of sunrise at an Indian village, with the curved blue piecing in the border representing running water." Barbara feels much can be learned from "the creativity and spirituality" of Native Americans, and she tried to incorporate the colors they typically use in their art. She especially enjoys working with geometric shapes in her quilt art. She loved working with the light tepees in the background, suggesting their presence rather than making them obvious. The unexpected surprise of the black-and-white border is something that pleases Barbara because of its "harshness or contrast and the movement that results."

As much as we would like to enjoy untouched nature, we live here and must share the earth. Barbara has effectively represented the theme of nature sharing the earth with man, giving nature the respect it rightfully deserves.

TECHNIQUE

Fabric Suggestions and Requirements

Cut triangles from a wide assortment of fabrics in each color range. Cut more than required to give yourself some design choices.

Background yellows and golds
3 yards (247 cm)

Reds, light to dark
1/2 yard (46 cm)

Purples to fuchsia
1/2 yard (46 cm)

Blues and teals to turquoise
1/2 yard (46 cm)

Yellows, light
1/4 yard (23 cm)

Cutting

Cut fabric into 3 1/2″ (8.9 cm) strips. Lay four strips together right side up. Using a 60 degree triangle or the template provided, cut triangles from the strips as shown in diagram 1.

Background yellows and golds
29 strips 343 triangles

Reds, light to dark
4 strips 41 triangles

Purples to fuchsia
3 strips 20 triangles

Blues and teals to turquoise
5 strips 47 triangles

Yellows, light
2 strips 18 triangles

Instructions

Using a design, place background triangles in bottom two rows of quilt. Using diagram 2 and the photograph as a guide, build pyramids from assorted fabrics in the color families listed, using pleasing depth and value changes, and place them on your design wall. Fill in with remaining background triangles.

Assembly

Sew two triangles together to construct a unit. Continue across the row. Finger press only! These are bias edges and they will stretch. Sew two units together and continue until entire row is complete, finger pressing, not ironing. After all rows are complete, join rows, matching points. Your top will be uneven on the sides. Use a ruler to straighten the edges, remembering to leave a 1/4″ (6 mm) seam allowance past the points of the triangles. Press quilt top gently, being careful not to stretch.

Many kinds of borders will enhance this top. The outer border on this quilt was constructed by drawing the entire design on a stitch and tear foundation, using foundation piecing for the straight strips. The curved pieces of the border were drawn on freezer paper, which was ironed on the fabric, creating a template, and then machine appliquéd onto the foundation.

Quilting

Quilt using your favorite method.

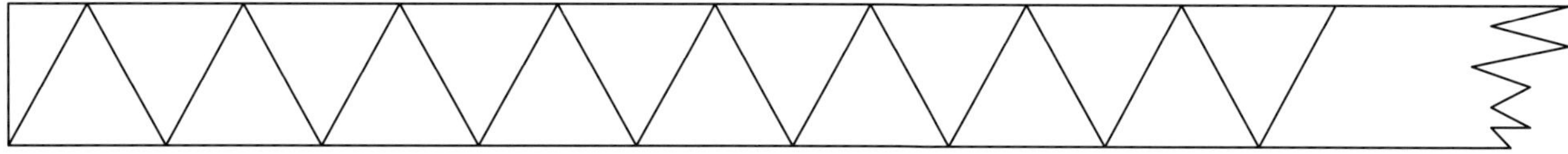

Diagram 1

Diagram 2

The Stardusters in Their Night Garden
Kathy Martin
60″ x 64″ (152 cm x 163 cm)
Hand and machine appliquéd, hand painted and dyed, machine embroidered

The Stardusters in Their Night Garden

My art is simply self-expression; something I can control to make it mine. I find nature, travel, our galaxy, and the diversity of the world's cultures very inspiring and often merge these subjects in my art. For years I made scrap quilts, but at some point, I realized there were art quilts and I changed my focus. Many of my works make statements about protecting our fragile environment and other relevant issues.

I like designing my quilts the most. I'm not very analytical, so I just put my quilt together and see what looks good until something clicks. Some of my best ideas come in the middle of the construction process rather than at the beginning, so I frequently enlarge my quilts to incorporate these ideas. I'm not interested in working in a block format because I find it too limiting. I'm especially drawn to the fabric and find the many choices intriguing.

Risk taking in quilt making is continual. To learn, you must incorporate new things in your work. I feel art is such an important part of life that there shouldn't be any rules about what is art and what isn't. When I create a quilt, I try to express myself and not worry about what others will think. I am complimented if others understand my work, especially if I am conveying a certain message.

Kathy Martin

INSPIRATION

Many of Kathy's quilts are inspired by nature and the preservation of the environment. The Stardusters in Their Night Garden, a glorious quilt, captures the mountains and waterfalls of the Pacific Northwest. Take a closer look; there is more to this quilt than meets the eye. According to Kathy, this quilt tells the story of the "hard-working stardusters who dust and polish the stars but find their workday world is becoming more and more polluted by aliens below." Can you spot the Stardusters peering from behind the bushes where they relax at night? Kathy has a wonderful color sense and her quilts sparkle with life.

Kathy created the appliqué mountains and the night sky by using the discharge technique, removing color from fabric using a color remover or a bleach solution. The waterfalls were created through painting, embroidery, scrunching, and beading fabrics. The appliquéd tropical flowers relate to her childhood memories of "spectacularly colored blooming rhododendron bushes in the Cascade Mountains of Oregon." Kathy used a large night-time sky border to "enhance the mysterious mood of this pictorial quilt" and quilted this piece by machine.

CHAPTER 3 Calming Waters

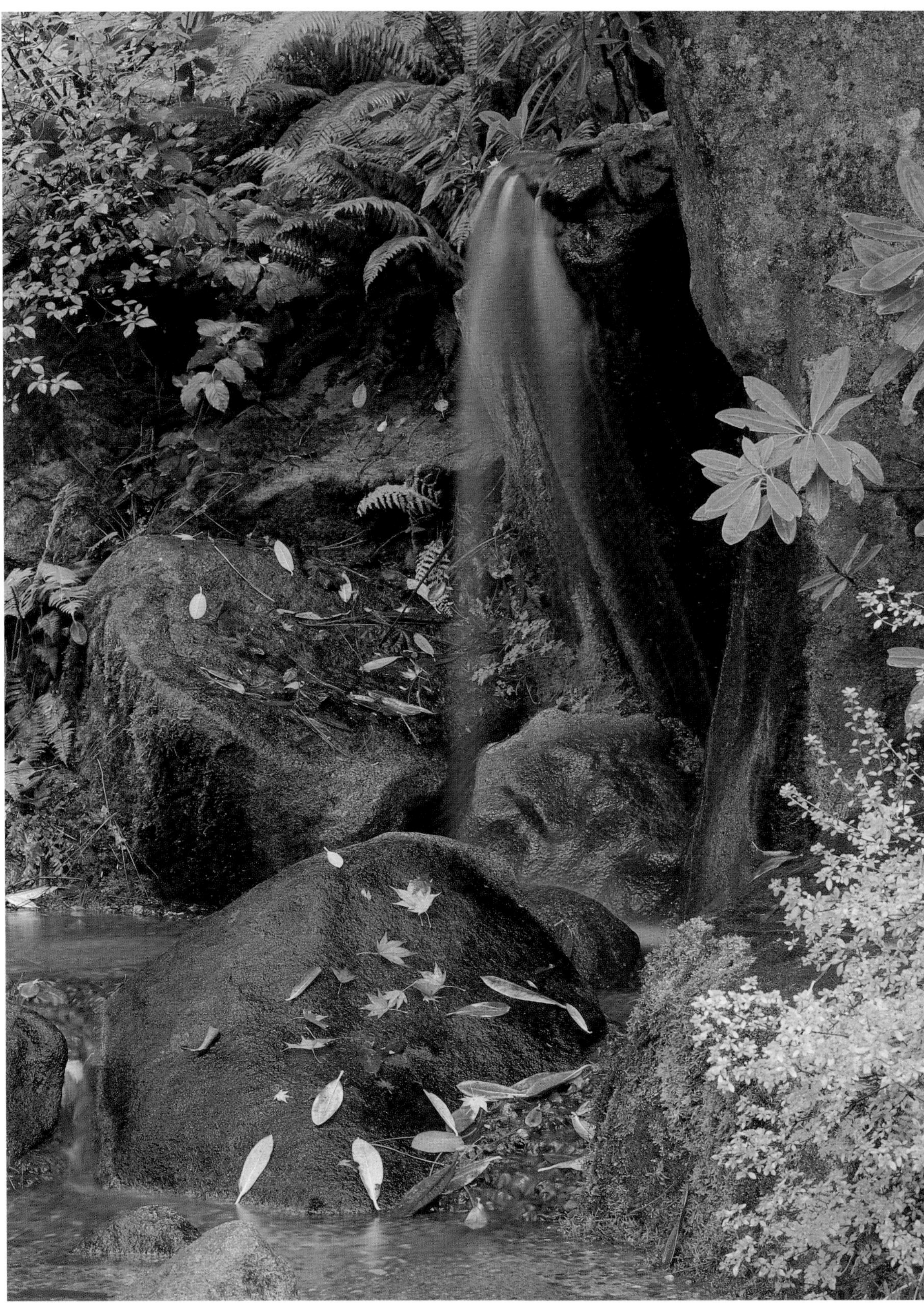

Garden waterfall, Washington Park Arboretum, Seattle, WA.

Stars at Ocean Shores
Connie James
46″ x 46″ (117 cm x 117 cm)
Machine pieced, embellished, stuffed, hand quilted

Stars at Ocean Shores

I BELIEVE GOD IS NATURE, and that is where all of my quilts come from. Quilting is a reward in itself, and I do it because it's inspired and I need to share it. You have to give back and share to make your life worthwhile. I create quilts because I feel like there's always been an art process in me that has not been fulfilled. I love working with color, values, and forms, and quilting allows me to express myself.

When I begin a new quilt, I just let the ideas come. I think that we are all messengers and that we should listen to our inner selves. Sometimes, I'm led down another path, so I just let the quilt grow and I don't hurry it.

I love using unexpected colors in my quilts and the technical part of assembling my work. My quilt art is all consuming, too much so sometimes. Quilting is exciting; it feeds on itself and just keeps building. The more I learn, the more I want to know. I'm never afraid to take risks because they give me the freedom of color and fabric choice. I let designs happen; experimentation is part of the process.

I enjoy throwing in a zinger fabric when I make a quilt and hope that when people see my quilts, they are surprised. I enjoy entering quilt competitions but winning is not important. I grow and stretch as an artist when I study other quilt makers' work.

Connie James

INSPIRATION

This quilt was totally spontaneous; the idea for it came to Connie when she wasn't even thinking about quilting. Camping near the Pacific Ocean, near Ocean Shores, Washington, Connie and her husband were fast asleep when their relatives arrived in the middle of the night and had to set up camp.

Opening the door to her recreational vehicle, Connie found the sky "crystal clear, like I could just pick the stars from the sky, and I thought to myself, I wish Joyce could see this, this would really be a quilt inspired by nature." Somehow, she couldn't push the vision from her mind, so Connie made the quilt. She says, "I wanted it to feel like the sky on that night and reflect the sound of the water and waves. I let the fabric accomplish this for me."

Connie stuffed the stars to make them the focal point. You can arrange this very versatile block to make quilts that appear entirely different. Experiment!

TECHNIQUE

15″x 15″(38.1 cm x 38.1 cm) block

Fabric Suggestions and Requirements

Select water fabrics that impart movement. Background fabric should be selectively cut if it includes motifs other than stars. Pay careful attention to bias edges in this piece.

1 yard (91 cm) navy
1/4 yard (23 cm) light blue
1/4 yard (23 cm) lavender
1/2 yard (46 cm) bright blue
3/4 yard (69 cm) turquoise

Cutting

Note: Cut fabric face up, not folded.

Navy background

Cut 24 each—Templates A, I, and J
Cut 2—11 1/2″ (29.2 cm) squares, cut diagonally twice (see diagram 1)
Cut 2—12″ (30.4 cm) squares, cut diagonally once (see diagram 1)

Light blue fabric

Cut 24 each—Templates C, E, and K

Lavender fabric

Cut 24—Template B

Bright Blue fabric

Cut 24 each—Templates D and H

Turquoise fabric

Cut 24 each—Template F, G, and L

Assembly

Precise 1/4″ (6 mm) seams are necessary for this design. Assemble the block, being careful not to sew into the seam allowance in the "Y" seams. See diagrams 1 and 2. This is one quarter of the block. Repeat three more times for one complete block. See diagram 3. Sew five complete blocks; leave one block in quarters.

Assemble quilt using large background side triangles and corners. Sew together in rows as in diagram 4. Attach border sides first, then top and bottom. Stuff center stars, if desired, before quilting.

Quilting and Embellishments

Quilt by hand or machine, using sparkling metallic and rayon threads. Refer to Resources for sparkling stars.

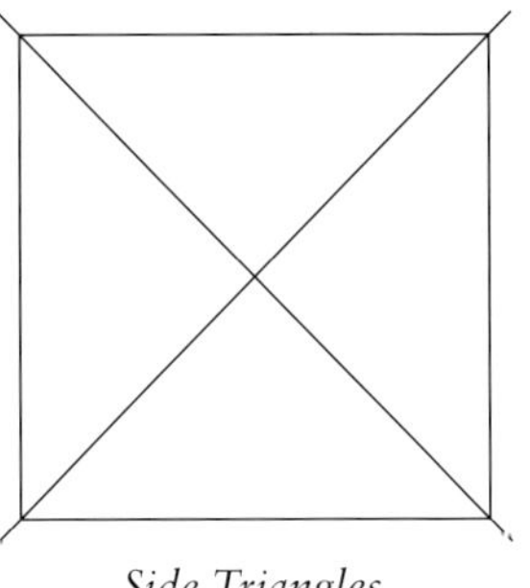

Side Triangles
CUTTING DIAGRAM

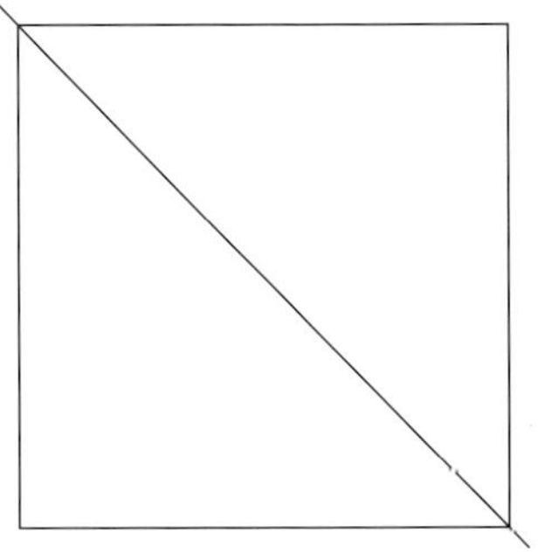

Corner Triangles
CUTTING DIAGRAM

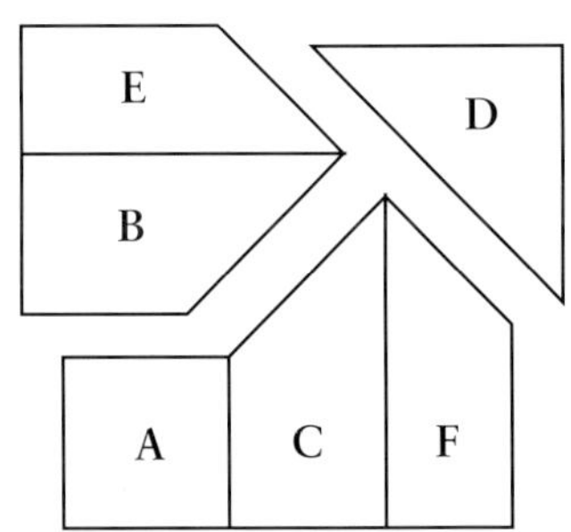

Diagram 1

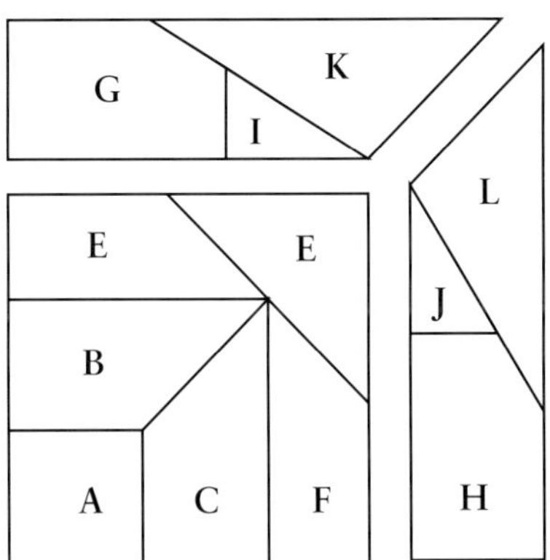

Diagram 2

Diagram 3

Diagram 4

Northwest Bounty
Joyce R. Becker
37″ x 36½″ (94 cm x 93 cm)
Machine pieced, hand quilted, easy watercolor quilt

Northwest Bounty

It seems as though my direction and growth as a quilt maker has made a complete turnaround since I began. In the beginning, I was timid and shy, unsure of myself, struggling endlessly over patterns, color choices, and so on. I never felt strong enough to just go for it and make my own decisions, so I relied on published patterns and asked friends to help me with fabric and color selections. I'm not sure when I crossed the line and discovered how freeing, uplifting, and challenging making my own decisions became. I think it was midlife. I have a theory that when you hit midlife, you either begin to take risks and do all those things you have always dreamed about, or you sit in a rocker, shrivel up, and prepare to die. The rocker route was definitely not for me. Giving myself permission to create without guilt or fear was the best thing I have ever done for myself.

I don't have any specific order or design process for all of my quilts. It varies according to the quilt. My design wall and my husband are very important factors in my designing. My husband can look at my wall and spot a mistake just like that!

The direction of my quilting has changed dramatically since my first quilt fifteen years ago. I used to be a purist who made only traditional quilts. Gradually, contemporary fabrics and machine techniques crept into my work. Now, I am willing to try anything once. If I like the technique, I use it again. If I don't, I just tell myself, "Glad you've got that out of your system!"

Joyce R. Becker

INSPIRATION

Northwest Bounty is an impressionistic interpretation of the richness of nature. In my Northwest environment I often see swirling, moving water surrounded by a lush carpet of greenery, with wildfowl feeding along the edges. Rather than a blue sky, I wanted the sky to reflect the warmth of a summer morning when the sun is not yet too high or too bright and it gently blends with the horizon, becoming one with the water. The richness of thick vines and blooming flowers growing wild, tangled and untamed, this ever-present abundance of nature, inspired me to create a tribute to the Northwest. Thanks to Northwest quilt artists Pat Magaret and Donna Slusser for graciously sharing their talent, skill, and watercolor quilt knowledge with me.

TECHNIQUE

Fabric Suggestions and Requirements

Select a wide variety of light, medium, and dark values appropriate for watercolor quilts (refer to Resources). Choose value first, then color. This work includes fabrics with dark backgrounds and large petals, medium value prints with smaller flowers, light values with small prints, and filler squares (mostly background) in all values with leaves or vines or small flowers.

Read the directions thoroughly to understand the specific kinds of prints you want. In order to accumulate a wide variety of fabrics, trade squares with your friends. The larger the variety, the better the blending and transition from dark to light value areas. Purchase small amounts of many fabrics or prepackaged two-inch squares. Purchase one yard of border fabric after your piece is finished.

Cutting

Cut 301—2″ (5.1 cm) squares of a large variety of dark, medium, and light prints. Selectively cut petal fabrics with dark background. Selectively cut filler squares.

Cut strips 5½″ (14 cm) wide for the borders.

Assembly

Use a design wall with a two-inch grid. Separate your squares into light, medium, and dark prints. Use a Ruby Beholder™ to help judge value and a reducing glass or peephole to see if your values blend. Assemble according to following instructions.

SECTION A Select dark backgrounds with large petals. Use different fabrics to form larger flowers, if possible. Use fillers to separate flowers and around edges.

SECTION B Choose typical Northwest ferns, lush undergrowth, and wildfowl squares in a medium value.

SECTION C Select water fabrics. Begin with darker values nearer the bottom, blending up to light at the top of the section. Choose squares that show movement and swirls. Look for blues that do not read as solids.

SECTION D This area portrays the sunlight softly shining down on the water. Selectively cut fabrics that blend pastels with yellow, blue, pink, and green. Large floral pastel prints work well, blended with other light-valued squares.

SECTION E This area consists of medium-value prints in a smaller scale than used in Section A. You will need fillers in this section, especially around the edges.

SECTION F These squares gradually blend from medium to dark, incorporating flowers with petals smaller than those in Section A. Use fillers around the edges and between flowers.

SECTION G This is a transitional section between F and H, using medium values.

SECTION H Using peach tones, this area flows into the light. Many filler blocks ease the transition into section D.

Take the time to play with the squares on your design wall. Transitions from one value to the next require blending. Use a reducing glass or a Ruby Beholder™ to help spot chunky rows that require more value blending. When you have a pleasing composition, take a snapshot. Your snapshot will tell you whether you have effectively blended your transitional areas and whether you have enough fillers. This quilt is 18 by 17 squares. Join squares to form rows. Sew rows together.

Border

Do not select your border fabric until your design is complete. Take your quilt to the fabric store and audition fabrics that read solid, but aren't. The green border fabric I selected has a swirling motion that suits the theme of this piece. Piece the border, adding a square that floats into each side. Attach that square to a 2″ (5.1 cm) strip of border fabric. Match and pin this pieced section to your quilt before sewing. Miter the corners.

Quilting

Hand or machine quilt using a variety of quilting threads (rayons and metallics). I used swirling movements in the water and directed sunbeams onto the surface of the water. Sunbeams curve around to the right in the peach area and to the left on the upper portion of the quilt. I quilted around large petal areas in the lower section of the quilt. Border quilting captures the swirls of the fabric.

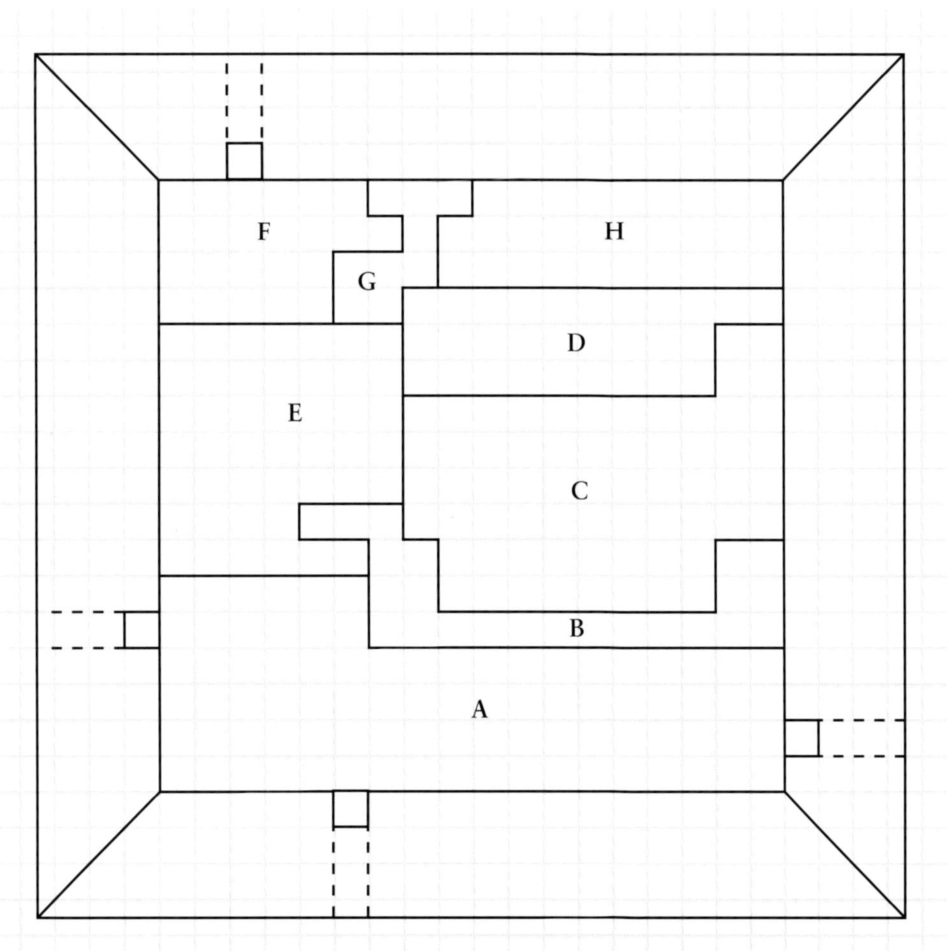

Assembly Diagram

River Rocks
Karen Perrine
59″ x 39″ (150 cm x 100 cm)
Hand dyed, dye painted, hand appliquéd

River Rocks

I CAN'T NOT DO ART in some form. Each piece of art is a challenge. Sometimes the challenge is in the design; other times it's the construction, or it might be the color progression. I want my work to be beautiful but not sweet. There is an edge, conflict, or contrast that I purposefully add. Sometimes these edges or contrasts are very subtle, so when someone catches them, it pleases me.

My favorite part is painting the fabrics. Sometimes I will paint a set of fabrics with dye and then I'll design a quilt from them. Other times, I'll design a quilt and then dye the fabrics. I don't like symmetrical things; I like my art to appear seemingly random versus patterned.

Painting the fabric gives me the most freedom in my work because it is spontaneous. Sometimes my painting is so wild I like the idea of making it more controlled yet energetic. The challenge is to make the fabric work in my designs. I like deep, intense color and extreme contrast in my art and intensely patterned fabric next to intensely patterned fabric.

I use my mind like a sketch book when I create quilts inspired by nature. I visualize my quilts but the finished project never looks like my image. I know it will change and I welcome it. I let the color and shapes talk to me, and I like the problem-solving aspect.

Karen Perrine

INSPIRATION

The first in a series of rocks and water landscapes quilts, River Rocks was inspired by photographs of a nearby river. Karen wanted her piece to reflect a "summery" feel—placid, with the light coming from the back to the front—so she painted her fabric with dye to reflect this mood. Karen paid special attention to the shadows from the rocks and painted them prior to appliquéing them. Karen says she is "intrigued by the challenge of portraying wet, slippery water and hard, rough rocks, with warm, soft fabric."

She advocates the use of quality dyeing products and uses cotton sateen fabric in her quilts because of the weave, the way it drapes, and the sheen. Check the Resources for products used in this quilt.

TECHNIQUE

Hand dyeing and dye painting using nature slides as a template

After taking slide photographs of rocks and water for more than two years, Karen chose two images that showed low water, pleasing rock shapes, and harmonious groupings of shapes. Once she determined the size and shape of the quilt, Karen drew the perimeter on a large sheet of paper, projected the slides onto the paper, and drew around selected rock shapes with a heavy felt pen. This drawing became the master pattern.

Next, Karen taped white cotton sateen over the master pattern and traced the shapes and shadows of the rocks with a soft graphite pencil. Then, she painted the water, including light and shadows, with Procion MX Dye, using brushes, setting the color by steaming her fabric in a standard canning kettle.

Using a crumple dye technique, Karen overdyed the fabric for the rocks seven or eight times to get a weathered look. Then, she traced the rock shapes (adding seam allowance) on paper and used these as patterns to cut out the rocks. Rocks were then hand appliquéd to the dyed water background.

For the leaves, Karen used a metallic knit mesh fabric that she stencilled with fabric paint, cut out, and hand appliquéd, using the paper method of appliqué. The branches for the trees were made from rayon knitting tape sewn on by hand. The rocks were hand quilted with separate, randomly scattered stitches, giving the feel of flat texture rather than lines. Karen machine quilted the remainder of the piece, matching her rayon and metallic threads to the background.

Midnight Sun
Kathy Martin
50″x 35″ (127 cm x 89 cm)
Machine pieced, machine and hand appliquéd, hand painted

Midnight Sun

I FIND NATURE very inspiring. You never know when something you see might spark an idea for a quilt. I'm intrigued by the sky, water, and mountains and use them in my nature inspired quilts. I often incorporate the sun as a design element, working with its luminosity. I enjoy the way light creates interest and reflections in my work, and I often work with landscapes because I am really drawn to them.

I think about my idea for a design for a long time. Then I put it on graph paper. From there I'll transfer my picture onto grided paper and then use graphite paper to transfer my design from paper to fabric, revising and enlarging when I need to. Often, I work with a muslin foundation so I can blend and stitch with the sewing machine, using machine embroidery and metallic thread. When I select fabric for my quilts, I have all of these ideas milling around in my head. I don't go looking for a specific fabric, but I have favorite colors I like to work with and a certain message I am trying to establish in each of my quilts.

I dislike giving up when I am designing a quilt that I don't know how to carry out. Occasionally I compromise or practice something two or three times. Most of the time, I find a way to make my idea work. It's hard, sometimes, to find the time to take risks and gamble in my work, but I learn and grow when I do.

Kathy Martin

INSPIRATION

Kathy often uses the sun as a design element in her quilts, as demonstrated in her subtle interpretation in Midnight Sun. Rather than copy a specific geographical location for her designs, she says, "I get a general picture in my mind rather than an image of a specific spot." She has lived in Oregon all of her life, so most of her quilts reflect the beauty of her native state. This particular quilt reflects her visions of the Columbia and Willamette rivers and the dramatic beauty of the nearby Columbia Gorge. She named the quilt Midnight Sun because "I long to see more of the sun during Oregon winters."

TECHNIQUE

Fabric Suggestions and Requirements

Follow the color photograph for suggested colors for this quilt. Water fabrics include gold and silver metallic lame. Consider using an all cotton iron-on interfacing for these fabrics. Using a new needle in your machine will help prevent snags.

BACKGROUND
1⅝ yards (149 cm) muslin

SKY
Variety of colors to approximate 1½ yards (137 cm)

WATER
Variety of colors to approximate 1¾ yards (160 cm)

MOUNTAINS
Variety of purples to approximate 1¾ yards (160 cm)

BORDER
1½ yards (137 cm)

Cutting

BACKGROUND
Cut muslin 52″ x 37″ (132 cm x 94 cm)

SKY
Cut strips in variety of widths and colors as follows:
Cut 9 strips ¾″ (1.9 cm) wide
Cut 8 strips 1″ (2.5 cm) wide
Cut 1 strip 1¼″ (3.2 cm) wide
Cut 4 strips 1½″ (3.8 cm) wide

WATER
Cut strips in variety of widths and colors as follows:
Cut 8 strips ⅝″ (1.6 cm) wide
Cut 21 strips ¾″ (1.9 cm) wide
Cut 3 strips ⅞″ (2.2 cm) wide
Cut 8 strips 1″ (2.5 cm) wide
Cut 3 strips 1⅛″ (2.9 cm) wide
Cut 2 strips 1¼″ (3.2 cm) wide
Cut 1 strip 1½″ (3.8 cm) wide

MOUNTAINS
Cut large appliqué shapes from templates

BORDER
Cut narrow border 2″ (5.1 cm) wide
Cut wide border 3″ (7.6 cm) wide

Assembly

Randomly place the various widths of fabric to achieve variety. Alternate sewing a new strip to the previous strip, left to right and then right to left. This technique keeps your seams straight instead of curved.

Transfer the drawing from graph paper to a full-size drawing on pattern paper. One square equals one inch. Trace appliqué shapes for mountains onto paper. Place appliqué shape on mountain fabric and trace. Cut out appliqué shapes, adding ¼″ (6 mm) seam allowance.

This quilt is assembled on a muslin backing. Place strip pieced areas on muslin backing first, trimming away the unneeded fabric that will go under the mountains. Pin the mountains onto the strip pieced background. Turn under and pin the edges of the mountains and stitch by hand or machine in a matching color thread.

Quilting

Machine quilt in the ditch, then add decorative quilting with metallic threads. To heighten reflections of the Midnight Sun, accent the mountains and water with pink fabric paint.

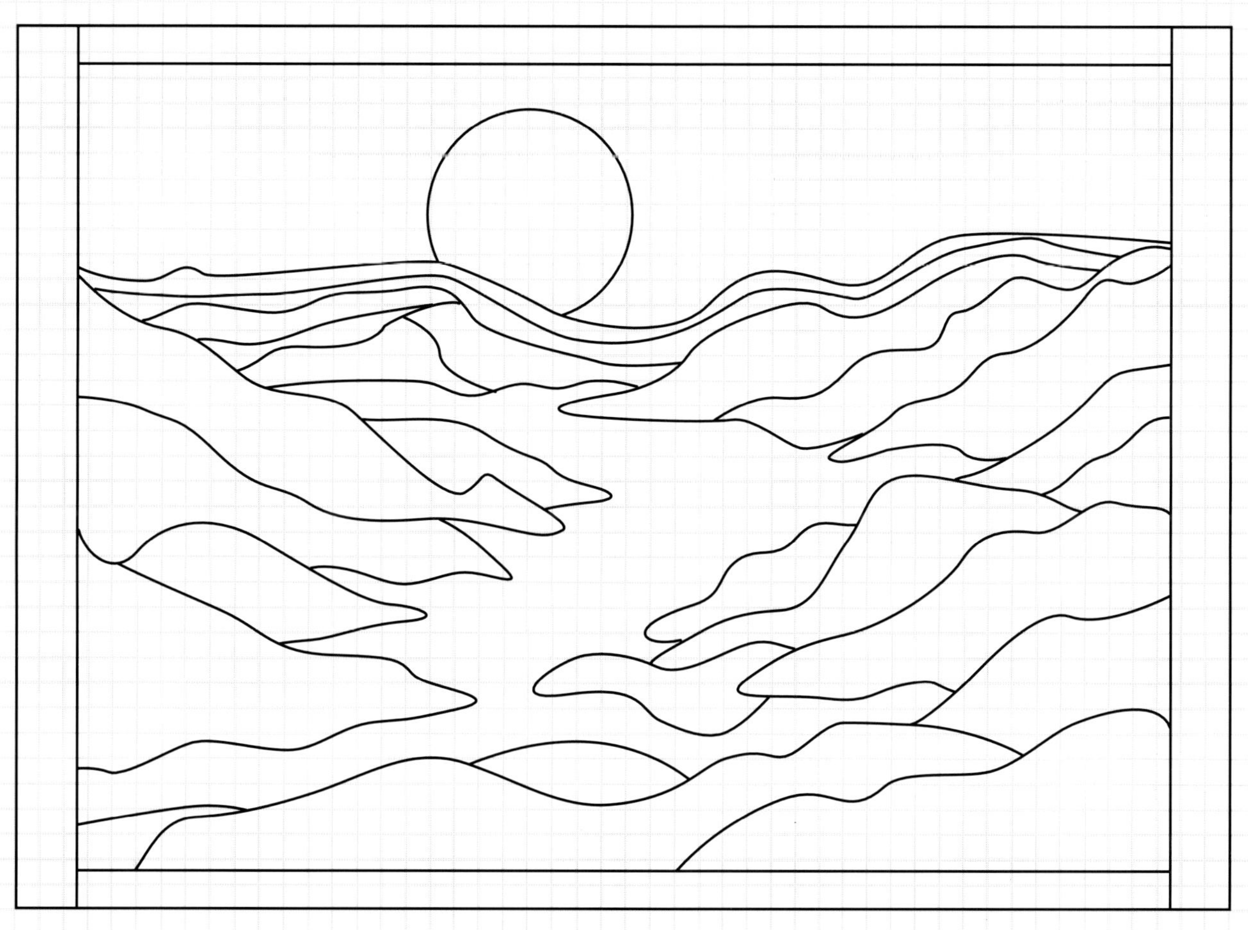

EACH SQUARE EQUALS 1 INCH

Fox Pond

Jane Herbst

70″ x 40″ (178 cm x 102 cm)

Machine embroidered, hand pieced, appliquéd, and quilted

Fox Pond

MY ART IS THE focal point of my life. When I create in thread and fiber, my design becomes alive; it really exists. I consider my quilt art more like illustrations using fiber and thread as the medium.

Machine embroidering the animals is the most interesting part of my process. I draw an image on a water stabilizer fabric and then put it in an embroidery hoop and machine embroider, sometimes using up to thirty colors of thread. After the image is done, I boil away the backing stabilizer fabric and dry it. I then machine appliqué the images to the background, using free motion and matching thread. I try to think of a good color scheme as I go along and pick fabrics for the background that reflect a particular texture in nature that gives the effect I want.

I personally identify with microscopic organisms most people have never heard of because of my background as a scientific illustrator. People don't appreciate the beautiful shapes in organisms, but I really enjoy using these unusual shapes in my art.

I do a lot of research for the concepts, finding out where the creatures live and what else is around them. I see my work as problem solving, as a puzzle being solved. Here's the assignment, how would you illustrate or convey this in a visual sense?

Jane Herbst

INSPIRATION

Jane calls this quilt a "natural science lesson wrapped up in a piece of art." She wants you to see both what lives above the pond and what's below the surface. Notice how the plant life and rock formations continue beneath the water and change colors during the transition. The branch extending beneath the surface is very realistic, as are the finite details of her creatures. Jane dyed the fabric for the underwater portion of the pond specifically so the viewer would have a bird's-eye view of her creatures and the other formations. Jane is currently working on a series of quilts with worldwide habitat themes, incorporating micro-organisms and unusual creatures. She tends to work with subtle, muted backgrounds and realistic colors for her detailed work.

CHAPTER 4 *Mystical Moods*

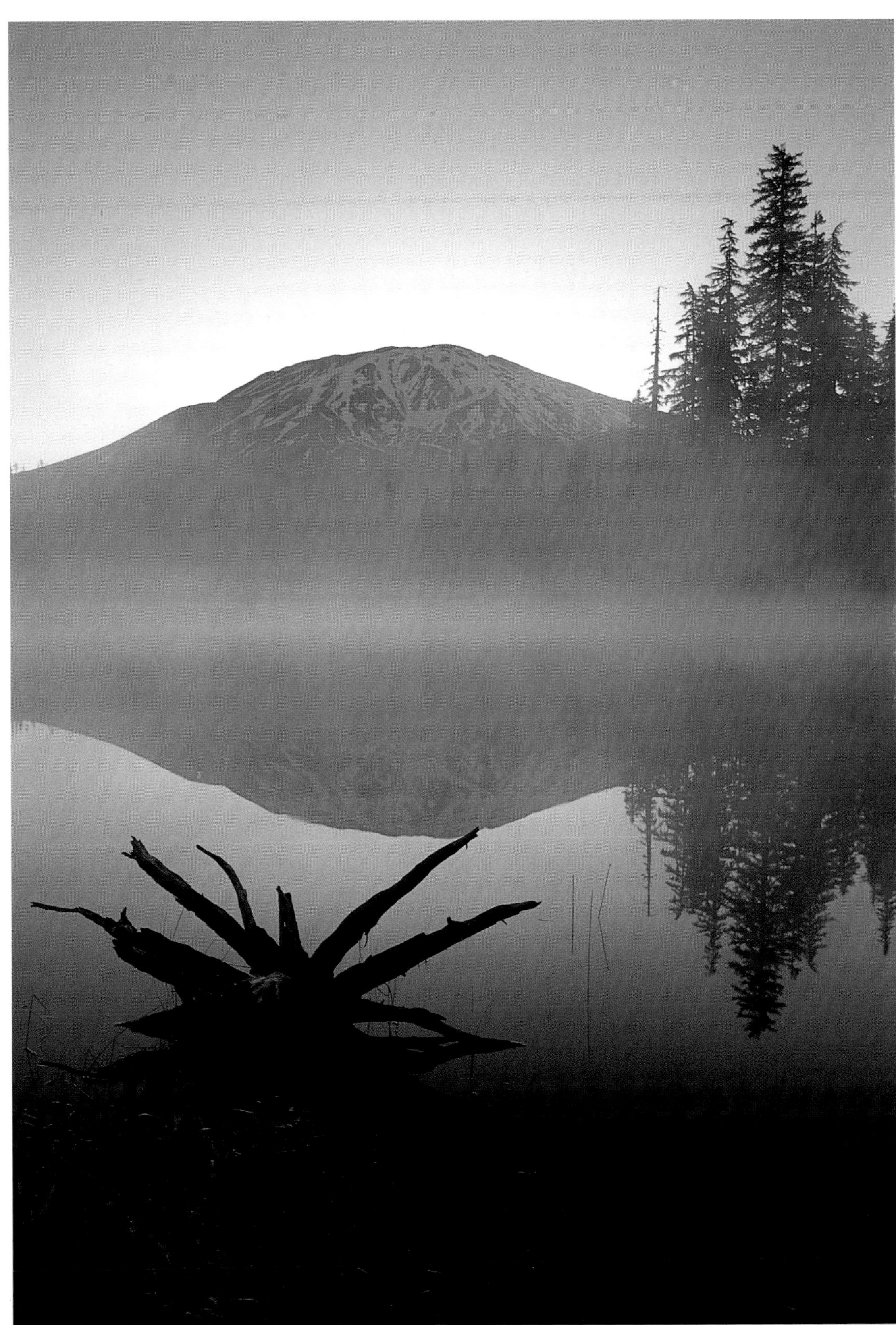

Predawn Mount Saint Helens and Goat Marsh Lake, MSH National Volcanic Monument, WA.

Falling
Roslyn Rowley-Penk
28″ x 46″ (71 cm x 127 cm)
"Toss and sew" strip and paper pieced, hand appliquéd, beaded

Falling

I AM CONTINUALLY DRAWN TO trees and autumn leaves for inspiration in my quilts. Perhaps it's because the falling leaves represent a final blaze of glory. Nature excites me. I like to experience how fall feels in the air, its crispness, and to hear the rustle and the crunching of the leaves. Once I have decided what I want to capture in a quilt, I do a pencil sketch, usually on the back of an envelope or some other scrap of paper, knowing that if my design works in black and white, it will work in color.

I am very passionate about my work. If a quilt excites me, it becomes all consuming; I get such satisfaction knowing I created it. When I envision a quilt, the first thing I see is the color. Then comes the design, expressing my feelings. After I have my quilt on my design wall, I jump around the corner to see if it works. If it works really well, it actually makes me salivate!

I think choosing the colors, touching and feeling the fabric, laying it all together to see if it works, is my favorite part of the process. Since I have an art background, I know the rules and I know how to break them. I like intense colors and my theory on color selection is to trust yourself.

I'm not afraid of failure in my work. Many times I will let my designs "cook," or "set in my baking oven" for lengthy periods to let my work become good.

Roslyn Rowley-Penk

INSPIRATION

Ros feels that each quilt "captures a moment in time" because the emotions you experience and the fabrics you use at the time can never be recaptured.

When Ros began this quilt, she specifically looked for fabric that would relay her feelings about leaves as they appear on the ground, no longer perfect or beautiful, incorporating the movement of the wind through her set.

After her foundation pieces were done, Ros put her piece away to "bake," and when she pulled it out again, decided she would incorporate leaves as they appear on trees or just falling, full of color. She added gold beads to represent the dew in the morning and gold quilting thread to add richness to the overall effect.

TECHNIQUE

10½″ x 10½″ (26.7 cm x 26.7 cm) block

Fabric Requirements

Background

1 yard (91 cm) unbleached muslin

Strips 30 to 40 fabrics

Cut ¾″ (1.9 cm) to 3″ (7.6 cm) wide strips in muted oranges, rusts, browns, teal, and purple.

Leaves

¼ yard (23 cm) for each leaf in bright jewel tones ranging from oranges, purples, golds, to greens

Border

½ yard (46 cm)

Cutting

Background

Cut 8—11″ (27.9 cm) squares of muslin for foundation of the background blocks

Strips

From each of the 30 to 40 fabrics, cut a strip ranging in width from ¾″ (1.9 cm) strip to 3″ (7.6 cm), cutting equal quantities of each width. I achieved this by taking the first fabric on the pile, cutting a ¾″ (1.9 cm) strip, then the second fabric was cut at 1″ (2.5 cm), and so on, until I reached a 3″ (7.6 cm) strip, then I repeated the process. If you are comfortable layering fabrics, you can speed up this process.

Leaves

Use templates for leaves, cut in desired colors

Border

Cut 3½″ (8.9 cm) wide

Assembly

Draw a pencil line across the diagonal of each square to use as a guide, so your strips will end up at the same angle from square to square.

Toss all of the strips into a basket and place it on the right side of your sewing machine. Place an empty basket on the left side of your machine. Randomly pick a strip out of the right basket. Lay this strip right side up along your pencil line. Choose another strip, lay it right sides together with the first strip, and sew along the edge (see diagram 1). Use a ¼″ (6 mm) seam allowance. It is important to randomly select your strips so you get a blend of fabrics and widths. Close your eyes and just grab! Press the strip back and trim the excess of both strips; throw the remainder in the left basket. Continue until the whole surface of the background block is covered as in diagram 2. When you run out of strips in the right basket, switch the baskets and continue. This ensures that the same amount of each fabric is used. Continue in this manner until all 8 background blocks are complete. Trim each block to 10½″ (26.7 cm) square. See diagram 3. Sew blocks in a 2 x 4 configuration as in diagram 4. Add borders and miter the corners.

Using the English Paper Piecing method, prepare leaf appliqués with templates provided. Cut 6 diamonds out of a lightweight paper without a seam allowance. Cut 6 diamonds out of fabric with seam allowance included. Baste the fabric to the paper as in diagram 5. Stitch the 6 diamonds together by hand, using a whipstitch as in diagram 6. Add a stem by cutting about 4″ (10.2 cm) of 1″ (2.5 cm) bias; shape the piece as in diagram 7. Arrange leaves and stems on the surface of the quilt as desired, and appliqué them to your quilt top. Be sure to pull the paper out of your leaves as you appliqué. Note that some leaves are not whole. Allow those leaves to overlap. Appliqué leaves that extend into borders.

Quilting and Embellishment

Use gold thread to quilt, and embellish the quilt top with small gold beads.

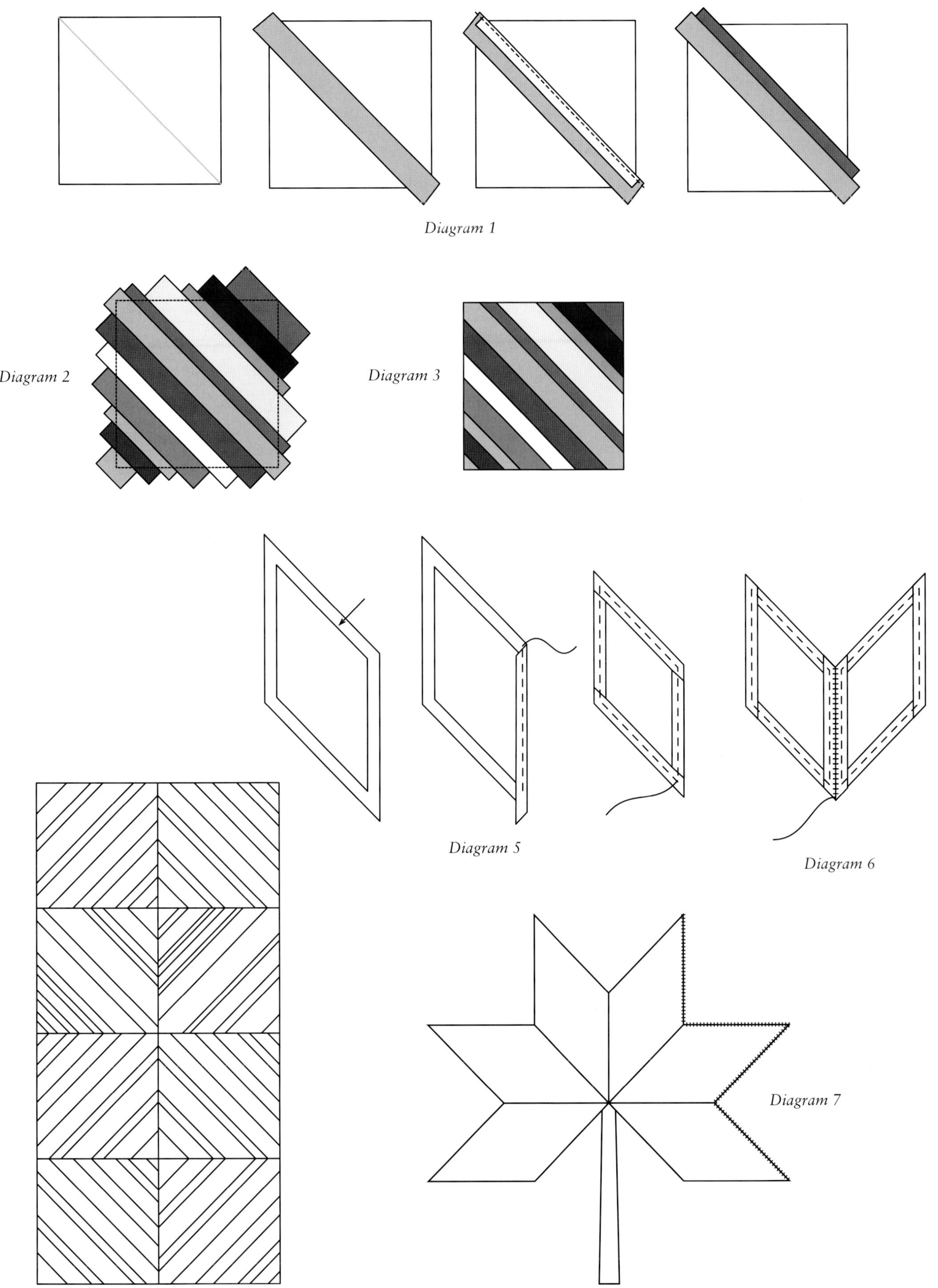
Diagram 1
Diagram 2
Diagram 3
Diagram 5
Diagram 6
Diagram 4
Diagram 7

The Nursery
Patti Cunningham
42″ x 42″ (107 cm x 107 cm)
Machine pieced, hand appliquéd, stuffed, embellished

The Nursery

I'VE FINALLY REACHED the point in my life where I just have to please myself in my quilting. I don't necessarily equate my quilting with art because my quilts are done for fun and whimsy and the need to satisfy myself. I feel flat without quilting; I'm compelled to do it.

I never adhere to a strict design when I begin a quilt. Sometimes I sketch my design out, but my quilts have to evolve as I make them. When I get an idea, I picture it in my head and reproduce what my mind sees. I love looking to nature for inspiration, and many of my quilts reflect this. Quilting feeds me; I can't express myself unless I quilt. It's like I let a secret part of myself out for others to see.

My quilts often reflect my mood through their fabric and design choices. Surrounding myself with my quilts calms me and gives me the feeling of safety I need in my life. They somehow connect me with the past.

I always do something new on each quilt to challenge myself. Timing is important for me when I begin a new quilt because I think there is a time when everything is right or in sync. If a quilt is forced, it doesn't work. A quilt idea has to jell and the mood has to be right for it to come together.

Patti Cunningham

INSPIRATION

The seeds of inspiration for this quilt have deep roots, going back many years to a time when Patti took a walk on a small, overgrown path that led into the deep forest in the Little Naches area of Chinook Pass, Washington. Along the path, Patti wandered into what she calls a "secret, very secluded room or nursery for baby trees, with the larger trees keeping watch over their children." She said that at first she felt like she was intruding but soon felt like she belonged, with an almost mystical feel enveloping her senses, where humans and trees have a spiritual link, coexisting side by side for thousands of years, each raising their young. The Nursery is Patti's vision of that mystical moment translated into fabric. Patti incorporated many textures and layers in her three-dimensional interpretation, and the quilt invites you to walk down the sun-filtered path, amongst the trees, to sit on a log, and enjoy the tranquility of the moment.

TECHNIQUE

Fun and fast three-dimensional designs on a pieced background

Fabric Requirements

A variety of greens from light to dark for background
A variety of greens and browns for trees

Cutting

Cut 441—2½″ squares from a variety of green fabrics ranging from dark to light. Background is shaded from light green in the upper lift to dark green in the lower left.

Assembly

Using a design wall, place squares so the light seems to filter from the top through the trees, getting darker near the bottom.

Appliqué

Mother nature is not perfect, and neither are trees. Use your own drawings for trees and limbs, mixing "baby trees" in with larger trees. Trees A, B, and C are stuffed. Tree limbs are layered and fringed, or layered and gathered. Some tree trunks are woven through the center of branches. Experiment with this process, mixing several shades and varieties of fabrics. Additionally, there is an appliquéd path through the forest, and there are appliquéd tree stumps and knot-holes on the trees.

Embellishments

Embroidery, artifical leaves and beads

Quilting

Hand quilt piece in #8 Perle cotton

EACH SQUARE EQUALS 1 INCH

Renewal II

Sheila R. Chapman

60″ x 60″ (152 cm x 152 cm)

Machine pieced, appliquéd, and quilted, stenciled, embellished

Renewal II

I CREATE QUILTS because I have to. I am drawn more to color than to the actual pattern of the quilt, so that is my starting point. Color acts as a catalyst and gets me going. When making color and fabric decisions, I pile my fabric in front of me and match the colors I see in my mind with what I have on hand.

I constantly look to nature for inspiration for my quilts. I notice things like shapes, patterns, colors, and the effect of light. I don't know if I do so consciously or unconsciously, but I store things away to use later. Usually, I try to capture a theme or a feel in my nature quilts. When I look at a sunrise, for example, I make notes to myself about the luminosity and shading.

There is a lot of passion in my art and I feel quilts can show all emotions, like loss. I'd hate to think of always being bright and cheery, probably because my life has had its ups and downs. My work shows the different levels in my life, the dark and the light, the highs and the lows. I incorporate these feelings through color. Sometimes it's hard for me to let people look at my work because of my vulnerability and because I have put so much of myself into it. I am driven to complete my quilts, to get them out of my head and create something I can see and touch. I make quilts for myself, but I'd like others to see the risk I take with color and fabric and perhaps notice something special in my work. If my quilts arouse any kind of emotion, I have been successful.

Sheila R. Chapman

INSPIRATION

Sheila designed Renewal when she was doing a lot of reflection about her childhood and life. She says, "I used it as a medium—an expression of affirmation and the path of renewal." In designing this quilt, she took her strength from looking at how nature renews itself through cyclical changes. Outside the window where she worked, there was a magnificent towering maple tree. She watched this tree, studied the movement of filtered sunlight through the branches and leaves, and watched the leaves change from bright emerald green to saffron yellow to flaming gold and russet throughout the seasons. To Sheila, this quilt is a seasonal representation of the changes and renewal both in nature and ourselves. This quilt was adapted and modified from a pattern by Gretchen Hill. Sheila incorporated a stenciled tree branch and silk leaves to bring her quilt to life.

TECHNIQUE

12″ x 12″ (30.5 cm x 30.5 cm) block

Fabric Suggestions

This quilt uses one block pattern in nine color variations. There are a variety of fabrics in each block, a different fabric for each template piece. Values read alike in each block while the gradation from block to block is stronger. The color sweeps horizontally across the quilt from lightest (top left) to darkest (bottom right), representing the maple leaf through all the seasons.

Choose a variety of fabrics in the following colors:

Light to dark peach
Medium coral to dark orange
Dark rusty orange to very dark rusty/black
Light pistachio green to medium avocado
Medium avocado to medium dark olive
Dark olive to very dark brown
Light yellow to medium yellow
Medium gold to dark gold

Instructions

Using the color placement diagram, select fabrics for the individual blocks. Choose the lightest colored fabrics for Colors 1, mediums for the middle blocks, and the darkest colored fabrics for Colors 9. Strip piece fabrics for Template B by sewing a variety of 1½″ (3.8 cm) strips. When you are pleased with the color arrangement, assemble blocks in the order shown in the construction diagrams. Sew seams in the direction of the arrows, stopping at the "Y" intersections. Sew the blocks into rows, and sew the rows together to complete the quilt top.

Stenciled Branches and Silk Leaves (Optional)

You will need freezer paper, 40–50 silk maple leaves in a variety of colors, small stencil brushes, a variety of fabric paint for stenciling branches and leaves.

Tape together two widths of 40″ (10.2 cm) long freezer paper. Freehand draw branches using branch diagram as a guide. Outline your drawn branches with a fine black felt-tip marker. Make a template for your branch stencils by cutting between the marked lines with a sharp utility knife.

Iron your quilt top so it is wrinkle free. On a large, flat surface, position the freezer paper branch templates, shiny surface against the quilt top. Iron a small section at a time, using the tip of your iron. Inside cut edges of freezer paper need to bond with the fabric. Use black, brown and olive green to paint the branches with your stencil brush. Repeat process for the right branch. When both branches are complete and dry, iron your quilt, using typing paper or a pressing cloth to set the paint.

Prepare the silk leaves by removing their stalks. Use a variety of paint colors to age the leaves. Dab color on leaves to make them appear speckled. Shadow around the perimeter of the leaf with another color. Highlight veins.

The silk leaves are attached to the quilt surface with metallic thread during the quilting process. Attach some leaves around the edge and others only along the veins of the leaf. Purchased silk leaves are durable and do not fray.

Quilting

Machine quilt blocks by stitching in the ditch. Carry out strip-pieced lines in Template B pieces. Quilt in the ditch around the entire square where four yellow Template A's meet in the corners. Draw large, loopy spirals across the surface of the quilt, representing leaves spiraling to the ground, and use a double needle to machine quilt them.

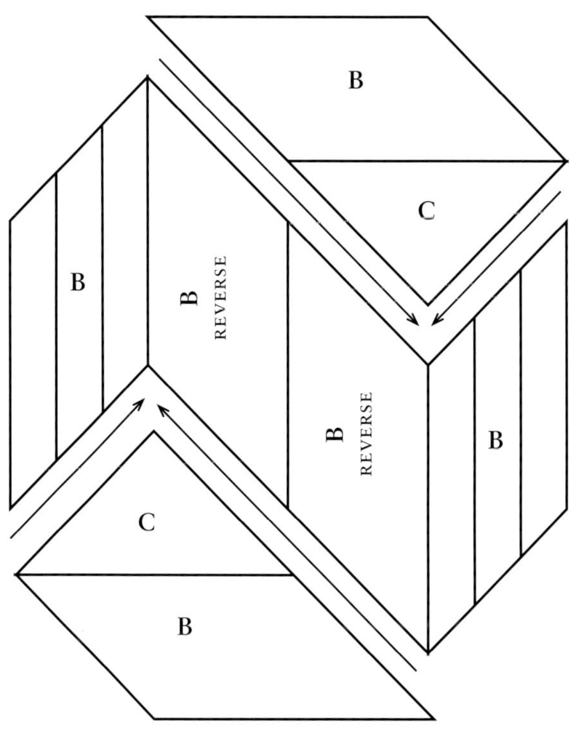

Diagram 1
CONSTRUCTION OF BLOCK

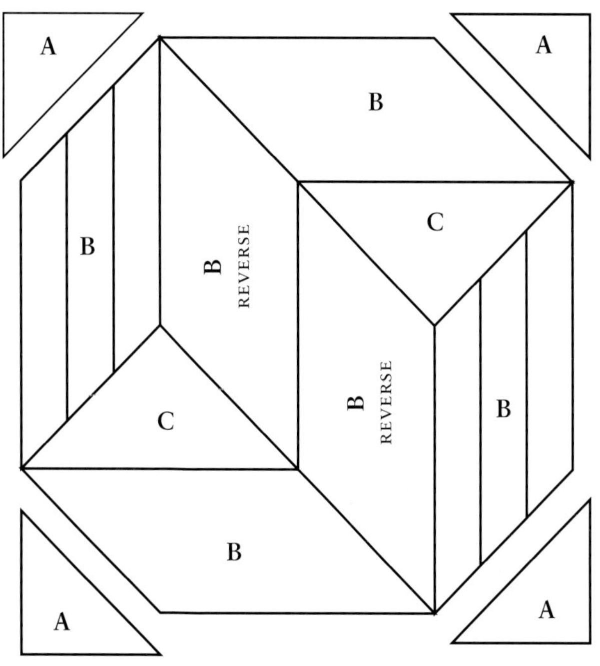

Diagram 2
CONSTRUCTION OF BLOCK

Diagram 3
COLOR PLACEMENT

Diagram 4
BRANCHES

Dreaming Pool
Rosy Carolan
53″ x 40″ (135 cm x 102 cm)
Hand appliquéd, free-motion appliquéd and quilted

Dreaming Pool

I FEEL LIKE WE ALL HAVE creativity that is an expression of our inner self. Most of us don't give ourselves the time to play and do fun stuff in whatever art we create, but we know it's there and we can tap into it and build on it when we choose.

For me, the inspiration or vision for a piece comes first. The most exciting part of the process of quilt making is in the original fermentation stage or gathering of the fabrics and design. I feel that is when I have the most creative energy.

I have always loved nature, whether it's plants, animals, or bugs. I have a deep love of flowers and growing things. The variety of color that we see in nature is astounding. The interplay of light and shadow have always interested me, and when I go into the deep, dense forest with the light shadowing through it, I have to tell myself, "I'm here, this is real." There's a reverence—it's mystical and the silence is inspiring.

I hope that people looking at my quilts inspired by nature have an appreciation for nature as a result. It's hard to admit it, but I want their approval. I do care.

Rosy Carolan

INSPIRATION

For Rosy, moving to Washington after growing up in Oklahoma was new and wonderful. During her first walk into the glorious Northwest forest, she came upon a pool of water. The light was bouncing off the pool and she said she felt enchanted. The cathedral-like feeling of the woods was so different from anything she had ever experienced that Rosy fell in love with the Northwest on the spot.

When she came across a note card painted by artist William Winden of Olympia, Washington, depicting a pool of water with leaves floating across it, the memories of that moment and her walk in the woods flooded back and Rosy felt compelled to translate these poignant moments into fabric art.

TECHNIQUE

Maximizing free-motion techniques and light and shadow interplay

By sketching her pond design on graph paper first as in Diagram 1, Rosy was able to do a value study where she "kept in mind the interplay of light and shadows on the water." Next, Rosy enlarged her graph to a full-size drawing and made freezer paper patterns for her water.

Using five fabrics, some reversed, for the pond water, Rosy appliquéd these pieces to a dark background using the freezer paper method. Rosy did not cut out the backs of the appliqué because she wanted extra stablity in her work.

Some of the leaf patterns in this work were made by cutting around actual leaves, while others were drawn on pattern paper to give what Rosy calls a "somewhat distorted appearance of leaves floating on water." Other leaves were simply free cut shapes. After she experimented with the placement of her leaves on a vertical work surface, Rosy pinned the raw edged leaves to the water surface, and attached them using a free motion machine technique, simulating the veins of the leaves with a variety of threads, including variegated. The edges of the leaves were not finished or stitched down because Rosy wanted them to "curl slightly as they do in nature."

Rosy free-motion quilted most of this piece, outlining groups of leaves, and advises quilters against stitching down the leaf edges. Her hand quilting in metallic thread captures the ripple effect around single leaves, giving the impression the leaf has just fallen and touched the water surface.

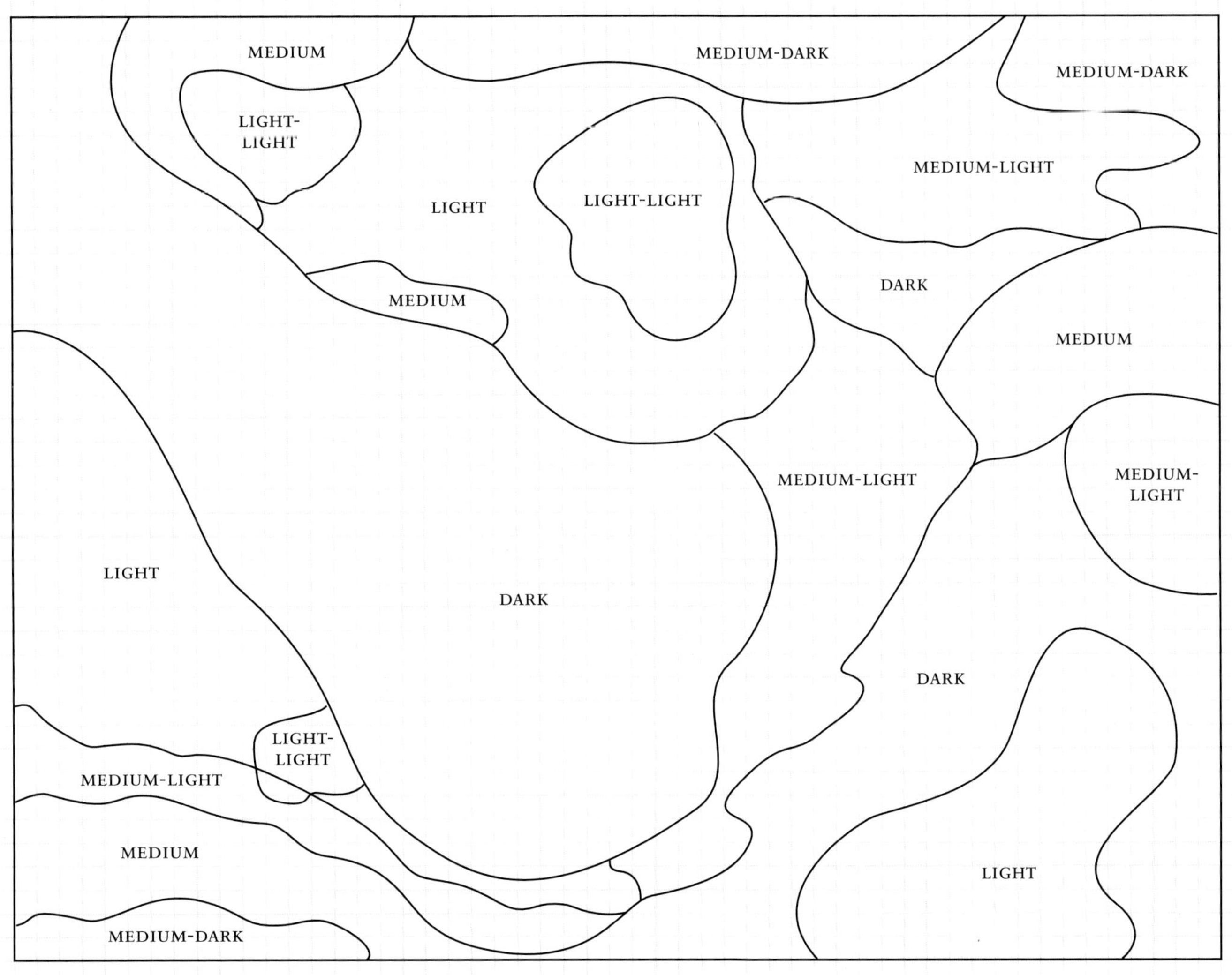

EACH SQUARE EQUALS 1 INCH

Metamorphic
Elizabeth Hendricks
40″ x 32″ (102 cm x 81 cm)
Pigment painted, layered appliqué, decorative thread

Metamorphic

QUILTING CHALLENGES ME both technically and physically because it includes design, math, geometry, and all sorts of things! I find it wonderful emotionally to find a medium where I can work things through and take them to their final form.

Color is integral to a piece from the start, and I tend to use everything, not shying away from certain colors. I see my art in terms of value and contrast, and I work color into that format. Sometimes the meaning of a piece dictates the range of colors I use.

I love playing with fabrics and the transitions that give and create movement or sparkle within a piece. My quilts that are inspired by nature come more from a form of experience, not necessarily something visual, but inspired from something inside me. The stimulation for these quilts might begin as something I see, but it is synthesized by my reaction.

When I am designing a quilt, I will often see a picture in my mind, but I'm not trying to capture that picture in my art, I'm trying to get the soul of the feeling. I don't skirt or dance on the edges of the energy and passion in my work; I get into it. I like to push and I love a challenge. I continually challenge myself to work on the edge, to try new things.

Many of my quilts have emotional ties because experience produces healing things. Making quilts pulls things together for me in a form where I can deal with difficult issues.

Elizabeth Hendricks

INSPIRATION

At first glance, the tie to nature in the Northwest might not be obvious in this quilt. Elizabeth incorporated stone-like fabrics into this piece that "spoke of places I have sailed, like the rose quartz beach of Cortez Island in Desolation Sound, and landscapes where I have hunted mushrooms with craggy outcroppings and boulders near the Little Naches Valley in the Cascade Mountains." After placing a pigment-dyed silk organza overlay over the entire piece, she quilted in marbled vein patterns. Falling rocks were then appliquéd on top, forming a third layer.

This abstract interpretation of an "earth woman," made out of granite, symbolizes for Elizabeth how everything that appears permanent and solid in life and on earth can change in an instant and become profoundly impermanent.

When Elizabeth designed this piece, she recalled the day Mt. St. Helens erupted. This once peaceful, snow-capped mountain—a legendary Northwest landmark—changed in an instant into a fiery volcano, spilling its volatile contents, altering everything that had once been solid and permanent, canceling all that once was. On a deeper level, the connection between earth and nature in this quilt relates to life in general and how we must trust that our lives will constantly move and change.

CHAPTER 5 *Inspiring Landscapes*

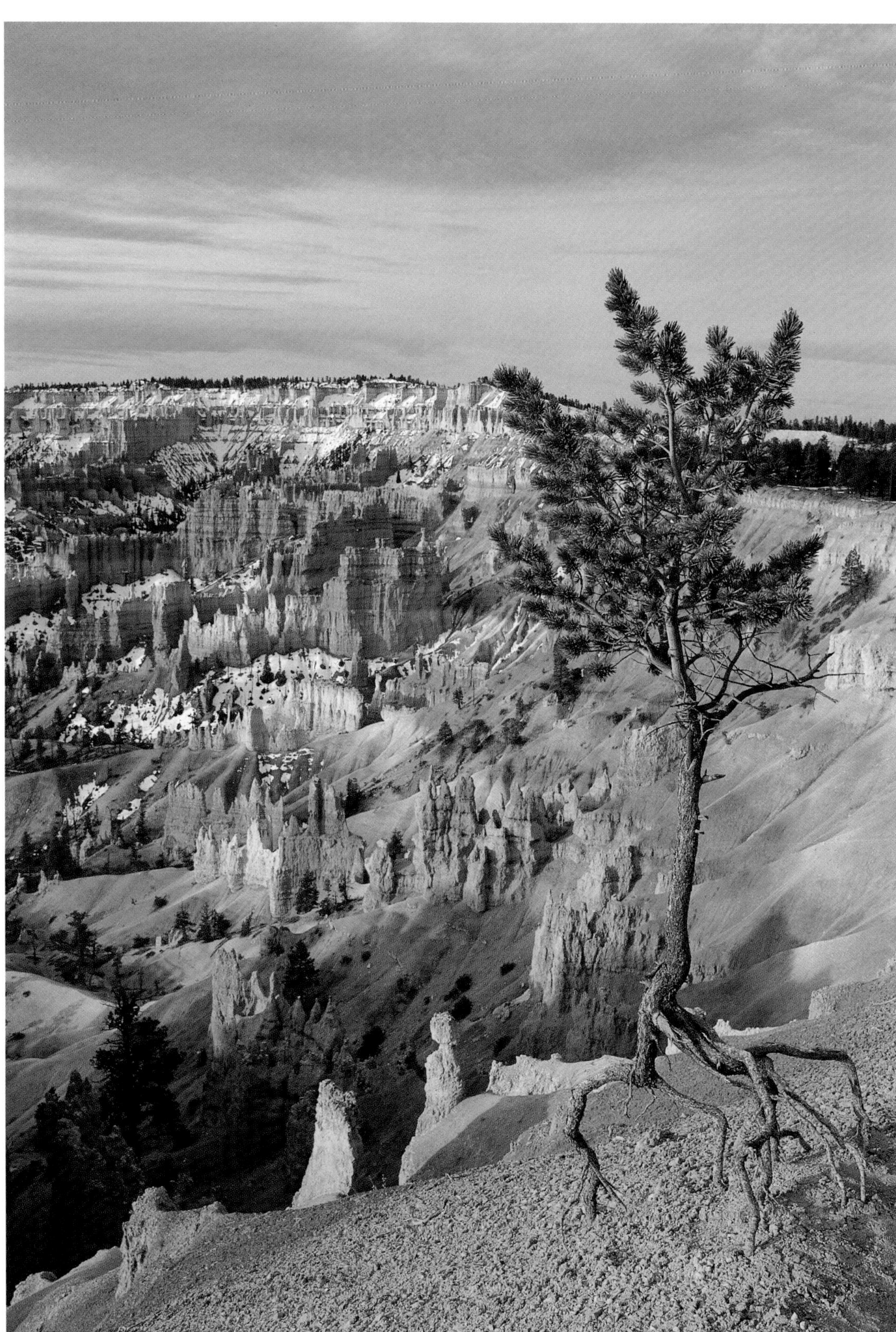

Limber pine at Sunrise Point, Bryce Canyon National Park, UT

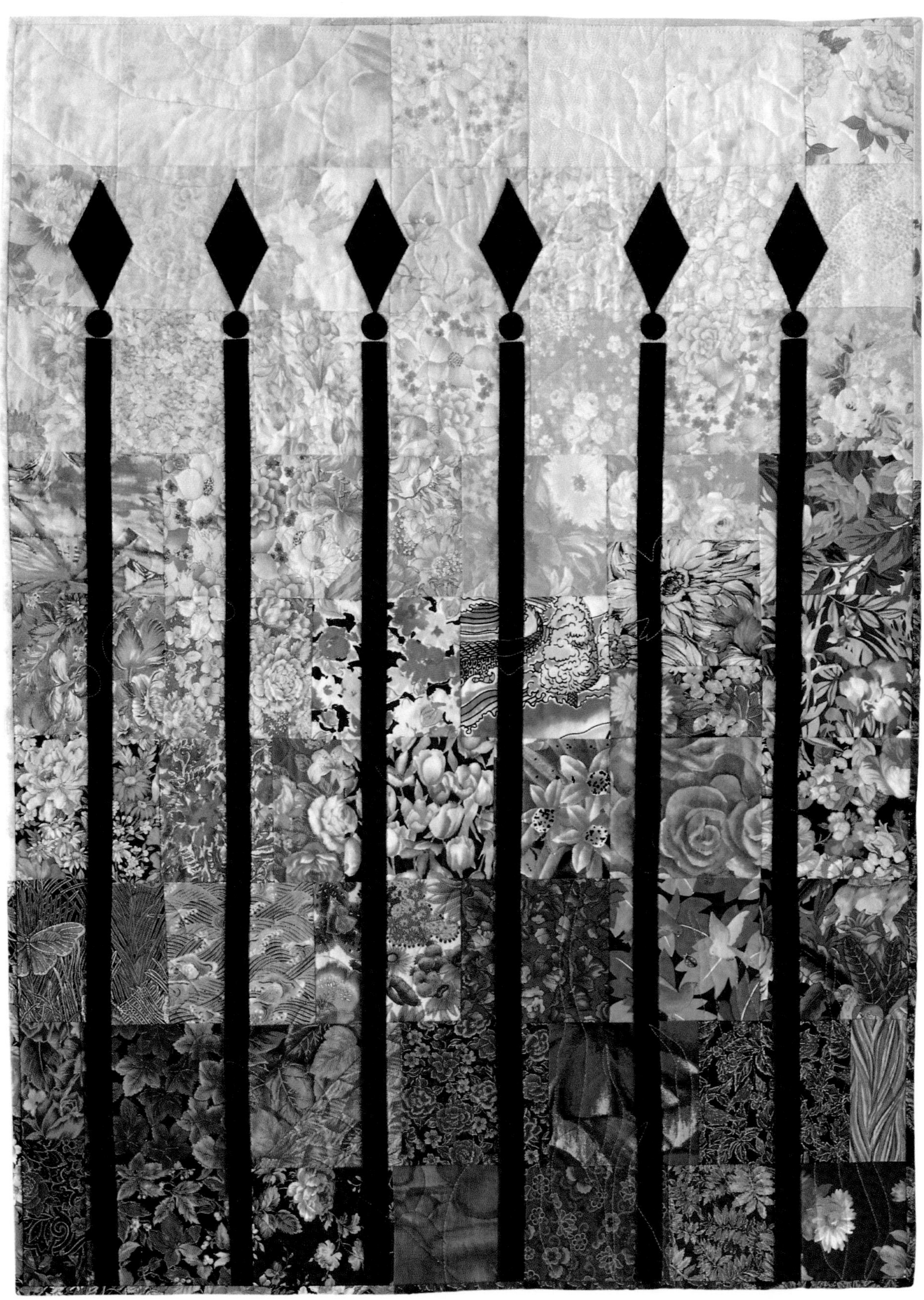

Urban Oasis
Melody Crust
42″ x 54″ (107 cm x 137 cm)
Machine pieced and quilted, hand appliquéd

Urban Oasis

I NEVER WORRY ABOUT the technical requirements in my work; I just figure them out when I get there. If I forced myself to think about how I'm going to get from here to there, I'd never start. I'm not interested in making the same quilt more than once, so I frequently set myself up with a new challenge before I start a quilt. For example, I like to incorporate things in my quilts that will be noticed from different distances. I try to be optimistic about life and I think that optimism is demonstrated in my quilt art.

I find playing with fabric the most exciting process of quilt making because I am a tactile person and I like the touch and feel of the fabric. Color is very personal and, in most cases, what is right is whatever works for me. I prefer jewel tones in my art, especially purple. I may glance at the color wheel, but in the end, I do what pleases me. When selecting fabric, I look for prints that typically have movement and that will support the feelings I am trying to convey.

I think the realization that quilting is an art form occurred to me when I first began studying older quilts. Knowing the facts and history behind quilting is important and I think it is up to us as quilt makers to educate the public.

Melody Crust

INSPIRATION

When taking workshops, Melody typically does not produce quilts in class but finds working at home in her relaxing environment, where she can put the theory of the workshop to use and create something original, more practical. After Melody took a workshop from Judy Warren, she came home and made this stunning quilt that expresses her feelings about gardens. Melody says she likes gardens that you can "see, but not touch"; she added the fence in her design so no one could pick the flowers and destroy the garden. Melody is fortunate to have a studio with huge glass windows in her home, giving a panoramic view of many of her neighbors' flower gardens and a gorgeous lake surrounded by trees. Melody frequently travels on photo shoots with her husband Charles throughout the Northwest, where she comes up with ideas for even more nature inspired quilts.

TECHNIQUE

This quilt is not based on the block format. It is an enjoyable exercise in selecting and piecing garden fabrics. However, for instruction ease, I have set it into a block grid. The bottom pieced section is cut apart to insert the bottom fence bars. The ornamental top of the fence is appliquéd to the top pieced section.

Fabric Suggestions and Requirements

Picture a garden in your mind. Does it have flowers, a pathway, a clear view of the sky? Does it include trees and grass? My garden has lots of flower beds, a pond, and a path. The sky is light blue with a shade of pink at dawn. Plan your own garden or follow the chart to plant mine.

Using diagram 1 as a guide, cut 63—6″ (15.2 cm) squares as follows:

A 8 very light blue
B 6 very light pink
C 4 light blue
D 3 light pink
E 4 medium green
F 2 pink to light plum
G 1 blue
H 1 light multicolored
I 1 blue-green
J 6 light plum
K 1 medium multicolored
L 1 yellow-green
M 1 dark multicolored
N 2 medium blue
O 4 medium plum
P 9 dark green
Q 6 dark plum
R 3 dark brown

Fence

From 1/2 yard (57 cm) black fabric:
Cut 6—2″ x 37″ (5.1 cm x 94.0 cm) for fence rails
Cut 6—1 1/2″ x 5″ (3.8 cm x 12.7 cm) for fence rail tops
Cut diamonds and round ornaments using the templates

Assembly

Join all of the squares in the first three rows to form the top section. Join all of the remaining rows to form the bottom section. Do not sew sections together at this point.

Slice the bottom section six times 5″ (12.7 cm) apart. Insert the long fence rails between the sections using a 1/2″ (13 mm) seam. Align the fence rails on the top section with the rails in the bottom section and appliqué them and the diamond and round ornaments in place. Sew the two fabric sections together to complete the quilt top.

Quilting

I suggest you quilt around your bushes, flowers, grasses, and other elements that make up your garden. Use your favorite threads to enhance the design.

	B	B	B	A	A	A	A
TOP	B	B	B	A	A	A	A
	D	D	D	C	C	C	C
	F	F	G	H	I	E	E
	J	J	J	K	L	E	E
BOTTOM	J	J	J	M	N	N	P
	O	O	O	O	P	P	P
	Q	Q	Q	R	P	P	P
	Q	Q	Q	R	R	P	P

Diagram 1

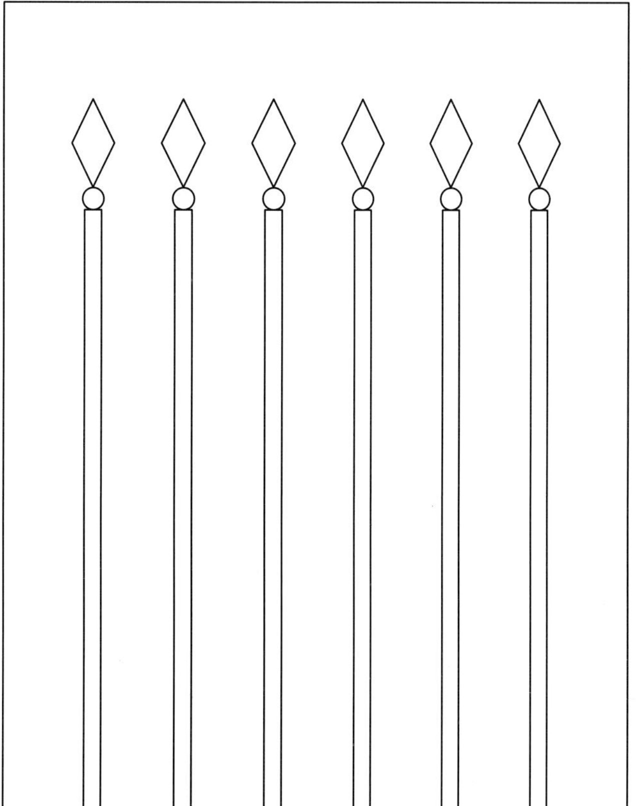

Diagram 2

The Farm

Ivy Tuttle

26″ x 37″ (66 cm x 68 cm)

Needle-turn appliquéd, hand quilted

The Farm

WHEN I AM out in nature, it is always interesting to me to see things made by people. When I was growing up, my father would take pictures whenever we were outdoors, and I always preferred the ones in which there was a person or an object in the distance, making the scene come alive. My quilts are the same. I always like to include people or things made by people to add that extra dimension.

Once I have the idea for a quilt, I mull it around in my head and it sits and stews for a while. I think about it while doing my everyday things, and gradually the quilt starts forming in my mind. Once there is a strong enough image, I start to draw. I use my sketch to make a full size drawing and use that drawing as my pattern.

I'm not what you would call a friend of the sewing machine. I do piece on the machine, but needle-turn appliqué and hand quilting is my favorite. I like the process of appliqué; it's relaxing and you can see things happening and the colors coming to life. I use colors I like because I make quilts for myself. They don't have to please everyone.

Quilting is something I would do even if it was forbidden by law. It's always there in the back of my mind. I work through a lot of things in my mind when I am doing handwork on my quilts. Quilt making gives me the freedom to be creative.

Ivy Tuttle

INSPIRATION

Unlike some pictorial quilt artists, Ivy does not use a muslin foundation for her quilts. For The Farm, Ivy began with the upper left hand corner and worked across and down in sections, appliquéing the pieces to each other. Ivy says, "I just love farms and country houses and I'll probably make more quilts with this theme."

Ivy enjoys making picture quilts because she likes "to visualize myself as part of the picture." The embroidered flowers and interesting fabric choices she used make this whimsical, pictorial quilt come to life. Ivy used a greeting card with a farm scene by Jean V. O'Brien as her inspiration for this quilt.

Ivy's philosophy of quilting is both refreshing and educational. Making quilts purely for enjoyment and relaxation, without regard for others' opinions, deadlines, or judging criteria, is something we all need to do to free ourselves up.

When was the last time you made a quilt for pure enjoyment, just because you found it exciting or fun? If we take this one step further, perhaps the "freeing up" step actually leads to the next step, discovery.

TECHNIQUE

A "no foundation" method for a needle-turn appliquéd scene

When Ivy makes a scenic nature quilt, her first step is to make a full-sized drawing to use for a pattern. She uses many design sources: sketches, photos, designs from coloring books or greeting cards, and then enlarges the design to the desired size, using an opaque projector. For this quilt, Ivy used a greeting card as an inspiration source. After she re-drafted and changed the design, she enlarged it to a full-scale drawing. Once she had the pattern, she traced the pattern pieces onto the right side of the fabrics. Ivy used a light box for this cucial step in the process and added a 3/16-inch fabric allowance around the drawn line. After the patterns were cut out, Ivy needle-turn appliquéd the pieces together in order, from the furthest distance forward. She sewed each appliqué piece to the next piece to avoid appliquéing to a muslin backing . This process eliminated the need to hand quilt through several layers. Ivy added embroidery details after her appliqué was complete and then hand quilted her work.

Wild Flowers at Mt. Rainier
Joyce R. Becker
Hand quilted and embroidered by Patti Cunningham
36″ x 38″ (91 cm x 97 cm)
Reverse appliquéd, hand dyed, pigment and dye painted, hand embroidered

Wild Flowers at Mt. Rainier

I Have Finally Come Home

As I look out my window at dawn
at the mountain standing tall and proud,
freshly dusted with snow,
it gives me strength to meet the day,
to try new challenges,
and I know,
I have finally come home.

I watch the wind swirling the brilliantly colored
fallen leaves, and I hear the evergreen trees
whispering in the breeze,
and I know,
I have finally come home.

I see my footprints traced in the glistening
sand of the Sound,
and I watch the gulls diving for fish.
I hear the gentle lapping of the water against the
shore
and a distant horn from an arriving ferry,
and I know,
I have finally come home.

Now, as the day draws to a close,
I am drawn back to the mountain,
awesome in its beauty, yet
surrounded in mystery with clouds misting and
closing in,
I am calm and at peace,
and I know,
I have finally come home.

Joyce R. Becker

INSPIRATION

To introduce this quilt, I have used my poem, "I Have Finally Come Home." It captures my feelings about nature and it inspired me to write this book. My quilt, Wild Flowers at Mt. Rainier, grew out of my poem and a photo shoot with nature photographer Charles Crust. On a crystal clear, summer morning, we hiked to the high meadows on Mt. Rainier, and the sight of the powerful mountain was so overwhelming it made the hair on my arms stand on end. The wild flowers in the meadows bloomed in the fresh, crisp air. I tried to capture the tranquility of that moment in my quilt to share with others the feeling of calm and peace that comes over me whenever I see Mt. Rainier. I always enjoy looking at this glorious mountain at sunset when the sky is full of color, so I incorporated that color palette into my quilt. I used both hand dyeing and dye painting in this work, and quilt artist Patti Cunningham graciously hand quilted and embroidered this piece, giving it depth and texture.

TECHNIQUE

Fabric Requirements

1¼ yards (114 cm) muslin base, cut larger than finished size
1¼ yards (114 cm) muslin for dyed wild flower fabric
1½ yards (137 cm) muslin for dyed sky fabric
1 yard (91 cm) muslin for dyed tree fabric
¼ yard (23 cm) muslin for dyed purple fabric on mountain
⅛ yard (11 cm) muslin for dyed cloud

Instructions

For hand dyeing and dye and pigment painting, refer to Resources for a reference book and recommended products.

For wild flower fabric, scrunch dye fabric several times, using several shades of green. To create the look of wild flowers, paint on fabric with thickened dye and pigment paint.

For sky fabric, tape muslin on a covered table and, using a small sponge roller, apply dye on fabric for sky. Blend colors with a roller dipped in water.

For trees, use two hand dyed fabrics. Dye first fabric in a dark green, then spray with bleach and rinse immediately. Over-dye the bleached surface with dark purple and black. Dye second or under layer of tree fabric with medium green dye. Bond the two fabrics together and cut out tree shapes. The fringed edge of the trees is achieved by cutting at an angle.

For purple fabric mountain appliqués, scrunch dye in shades of purple.

For cloud appliqué, scrunch dye fabric in a pink color and paint over surface with a pearlized white fabric pigment.

Assembly

Pin 38″ x 40″ (97 cm x 102 cm) white muslin backing on design wall. Sketch mountain shape on pattern paper. Trace mountain shape on sky fabric. Place sky fabric on top of muslin. Baste. Using reverse appliqué, cut away sky fabric, revealing white muslin mountain shape. Using the same procedure, complete wild flower section in reverse appliqué. Return the design to the working wall and place the trees. Appliqué trees by hand or machine. Randomly cut and place purple shaded areas on mountain. Appliqué shapes. Cut desired shape for cloud, appliqué and stuff. Refer to *Appliqué! Appliqué!! Appliqué!!!* listed in Resources for more detailed appliqué instructions.

Quilting and Embellishments

Add texture and dimension to the mountain with quilting and embroidery. Use threads that pick up the hues of the sky and the mountain. The sky is quilted in cloud shapes with a variety of colored rayon and quilting threads. To add texture to the wild flowers, French knots are used throughout. Hot Fix™ stones are used in the sky for sparkling stars (see Resources).

Assembly Diagram
EACH SQUARE EQUALS 1 INCH

Flowers in the Mist
Charlene Phinney
54″ x 49″ (137 cm x 124 cm)
Machine pieced, hand quilted, using a design wall

Flowers in the Mist

CREATING QUILTS is the only way I can release my artistic ability. I think doing anything artistic is taking a risk. Some people won't understand your art, so you automatically set yourself up for criticism. You've got to be able to accept criticism because not everyone will like everything you do. What you think is important.

When I design a quilt inspired by nature, the idea sits in the back of my mind and I know what I want to portray, yet I want it to be subtle. Some people get my theme; others don't.

I most like creating and designing the piece itself. I like the feel of fabrics and having the colors turn into something that they weren't. When I start something, I often go off on tangents I never expected. I don't work in a certain order when I make a quilt. I'll see a fabric and it will say, "Start with me." I let the fabric tell me what it wants to do, then I start hacking up fabric and putting it on the wall. I don't believe in staying within certain confines; it's terrible to feel structured, so I just go for it.

It's hard to explain the emotions behind my quilts. I just do a certain quilt because it has to be done. If I am in a down mood, I might work on something bright and release some frustrations. Things will be better the next day.

Charlene Phinney

INSPIRATION

This quilt represents "the calming feel of flowers in the mists and rains of the Pacific Northwest, a tranquility that I love." Charlene designed this quilt because she wanted to show that beautiful flowers and plants can survive in our Northwest climate, reborn in a form of renewal and new growth when the sun finally makes an appearance. She used Japanese fabrics with "a misty feel" and "soft flowers." The lively sashing areas in this quilt convey "the riot of colors in springtime flowers."

Charlene used several thicknesses of varied threads for most of her hand quilting and invented a clever way of tying knots on the top of the quilt, leaving a small tail, and unraveling the thread so it appears to be an embellishment.

TECHNIQUE

Fabric Suggestions

Select several Japanese fabrics, fabrics with a misty feel and/or fabrics with soft flowers in muted color families that appeal to you. Add a bright color for accent.

Designing

The secret to this quilt is using your design wall and working in rows. Start with a favorite piece of fabric and place it on your design wall. Visualize it cut in different areas. If cutting frightens you, move white paper over the surface of the fabric to block out areas of the print. Let your inner eye tell you what looks exciting. Then cut your fabric to a size that feels right, adding seam allowances. The first piece you cut is the hardest. You will be working on all the rows at the same time, moving from area to area. Use solids in areas where you would like to do some decorative hand quilting. Keep your eye flowing around the quilt top. You can use standard quilt blocks—simple nine patches, checkerboards, or half-square triangles—in the rows. See diagram 1 for the layout I used. If you are more comfortable drawing the quilt design first, refer to *Calico and Beyond* listed in Resources.

Assembly

Row 1 Large rectangles are used in this row. The crazy patch block is made by starting with a five-sided shape and surrounding it with a variety of strip widths.

Row 2 This row has two long edges, one on each side, in different widths. The center area is made of strips that are sewn together, cut in various widths, then sewn together again. The placement of the color was changed by flipping sections. The bright colored angled strips create the design accent.

Row 3 Large rectangles and strips are used in this row. This is a good row to start in.

Row 4 This row is made up of flying geese and a square-in-a-square. The geese are Templates A and B and the square-in-square are Templates B and C. Make as many as you need for the length of your row. The longer triangles are made with Templates D, E, F, and G. See diagram 2.

Row 5 Checkerboards and large floral pieces dominate this row.

Row 6 This narrow row is made of strips and triangles. Triangles are made from Template H. You can use prairie points instead of triangles, if desired. See diagram 3.

Row 7 Checkerboards, a crazy patch block, and strips of various widths make up this row.

The borders of this quilt are made from a variety of widths. The bright strip angles were achieved by extending the inner row angles. Use the same angle to help keep the design in control and not add conflicting eye movement, since the central angles are very strong. The small red border on the left is sewn in as an empty cording case. Use your own judgment for size determinations.

Quilting

Now it's time to enjoy your quilt top. Let the quilt tell you what to stitch. Each section can be worked as an independent unit. Some design elements are repeated to keep the quilt coherent. You can use #8 Perle cotton, rayon embroidery thread, Brazilian embroidery thread, and metallic thread for quilting. Perle cotton stitches can be longer than normal quilting stitches as long as they are evenly spaced. Leave some of the knots on the top surface for design interest. Embellish with beads and buttons, if desired.

Diagram 1

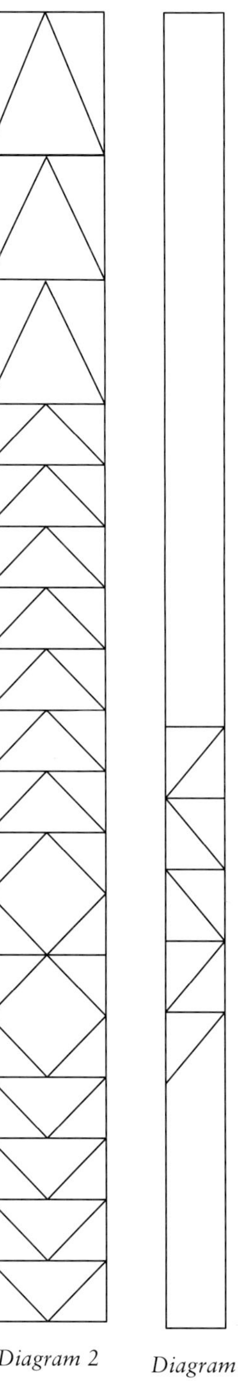

Diagram 2 *Diagram 3*

Mt. Shuksan–Shalom
Karen Schoepflin Hagen
86″ x 96″ (218 cm x 244 cm)
Needle turn and machine appliquéd, machine pieced, hand quilted

Mt. Shuksan—Shalom

MY QUILTS ARE PICTURES in my mind that I try to express in fabric to evoke some sort of feeling. I am a nature person and I would spend all of my time outside if I had the chance. I try to capture certain effects from nature in sketches because they are so fleeting.

My art is an extension or an expression of myself in a medium, and I approach it that way. I don't feel it is my burden to convince others that quilting is an art form, but it is my burden to share my art. Quilting is the most important thing to me. It seems that everywhere I look, the more I see and the more I want to do.

I look at quilting as a challenge and I find it a joy to mix techniques, not knowing how my finished piece will turn out. I love having a variety of things to choose from for themes for my quilts. I am very spontaneous when I am designing but I do pay attention to the detail and finishing of my pieces.

I don't believe in rules and I take risks all the time when I make quilts. I always do my best effort, technically, but my focus stays on the idea or design and the overall picture I want to present. When I watch people looking at my quilts, I always like it when they don't say anything. I get pretty wordless myself when I see quilts that really touch me, so I figure it's a compliment when someone just looks at my art without speaking.

Karen Schoepflin Hagen

INSPIRATION

Karen layered many fabrics in this piece and used frayed denim for the boughs of many of her trees. She sought out denims that were green with black in them, cut out her shapes, and then threw them in the washer and dryer several times so they would fray. When they came out of the dryer, she says, "They looked like a bunched up mess," but after she ironed them and sewed them to her quilt, they made it appear painted with fabric. Karen even saved the frayed threads from her dryer vent and used them for part of the ground cover on this quilt. Karen enjoys incorporating her love of nature in her quilt art. She refuses to have a deadline for her work and says "it would ruin the enjoyment of the quilt."

CHAPTER 6 The Richness of Life

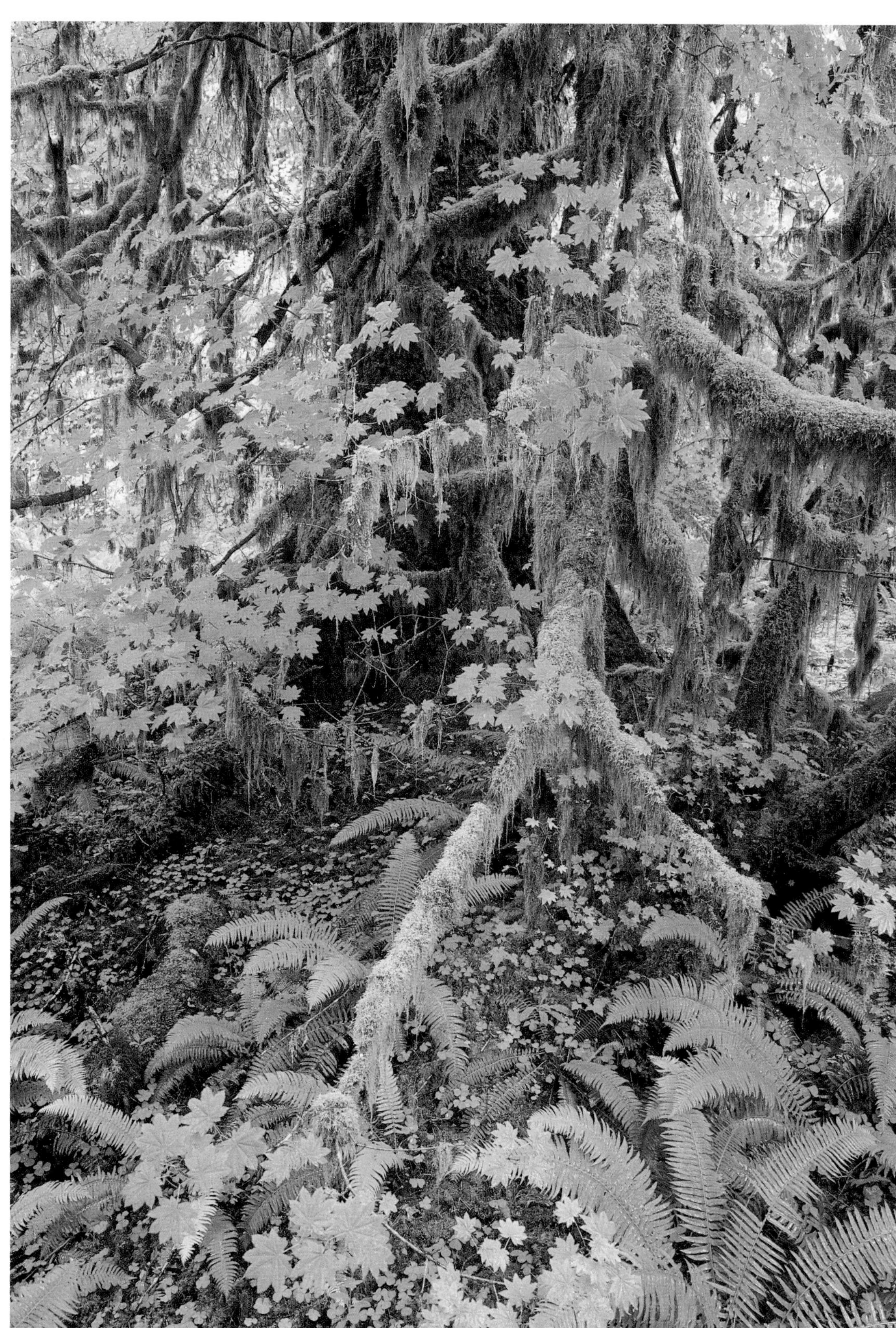

Giant spruce, moss and lush foliage, Quinault Rain Forest, Olympic National Park, WA.

Evergreen Habitat
Flo Burghardt
Machine quilted by Sue Smith
71″ x 71″ (180 cm x 180 cm)
Machine pieced, animal prints overdyed

Evergreen Habitat

I CREATE QUILTS because I love color and putting things together. I get inspired by fabric but the color always gets me first. Even when I try to make a quilt that is quiet and subdued, it comes out bright and alive.

When I am designing a quilt, I usually have a specific purpose for making it. I love using nature themes in my art because there are so many intriguing manifestations around me. I love the wheat fields, the mountains, the water, and the greenery. I believe I am unconsciously aware of shapes in nature.

There is a lot of passion in my quilting. I can't do a little bit and just put it away. I have to do it all, start to finish; I'm absolutely driven when I start a quilt. A tension builds in me when I start piecing. Technically, my quilts have to be precise; I am really fussy. I measure three times and cut once. I want it to just fall together. My precision is part of my creative energy. Every quilt I do is an experiment and a learning process. If it goes badly, I throw it away. It never worries me. To me, quilting is an art form, and I think that most people would agree, whether they are knowledgeable about quilt art or not. Quilts are timeless, so people identify with them. When people look at my quilt art, the only thing I hope for is to hear a quick intake of breath because it has been taken away!

Flo Burghardt

INSPIRATION

This quilt is a "preservation quilt," affirming Flo's feelings that "the Northwest is home. I live here and we need to preserve the things that make it so spectacular and beautiful." Flo used an animal theme in this quilt to "show them respect, or pay tribute to them." Flo selected the preprinted animal fabric because the animals seemed to "look you in the eye." She overdyed this fabric to add the flavor of the Northwest climate and mood. The greens represent the evergreens and the blues represent the water and gray skies. The flying geese blocks suggest mountains or flying birds.

I included this quilt in the book because so many fabrics printed with animals, birds, and nature scenes are readily available to quilters. Incorporating these fabrics into your quilts to make a statement of what you love is important. Find a panel of fabric that incorporates your love of nature and use or adapt the design Flo has furnished to create your one-of-a-kind tribute.

TECHNIQUE

Fabric Requirements

NINE PATCH BLOCKS
- 1/2 yard (46 cm) silvery, snowy print
- 3/4 yard (69 cm) medium blue print
- 3/4 yard (69 cm) medium green print
- 1 yard (91 cm) small animal prints for centers

LOG CABIN BLOCKS
- 2 yards (183 cm) of a variety of green prints ranging from light to dark
- 2 yards (183 cm) of a variety of blue prints ranging from light to dark
- 1 yard (91 cm) large animal print with border
- 1/2 yard (46 cm) medium animal print
- 1/2 yard (46 cm) small animal print

BACKGROUND FOR FLYING GEESE
- 1/2 yard (46 cm) pale blue solid
- 1/2 yard (46 cm) pale green solid

GEESE
- Variety of light to dark prints in both blue and green

BORDER
- 1 1/2 yards (137 cm) dark blue print
- 1 1/2 yards (137 cm) dark green print

Cutting

Cut 3 1/2″ (8.9 cm) squares for nine patch blocks
Cut log cabin strips 1 3/4″ x 42″ (4.4 cm x 107 cm)
Cut flying geese using Templates A and B
Cut large animal prints 8 1/2″ (21.6 cm) square
Cut medium animal prints 4 1/2″ x 4" (11.4 cm x 10.2 cm)
Cut small animal prints 3 1/2″ (8.9 cm) square
Cut border animal panels as needed

Assembly

Follow the diagrams and make the appropriate number of blocks. Assemble blocks as shown. Refer to the diagram for border treatment.

Quilting

Machine or hand quilt as desired.

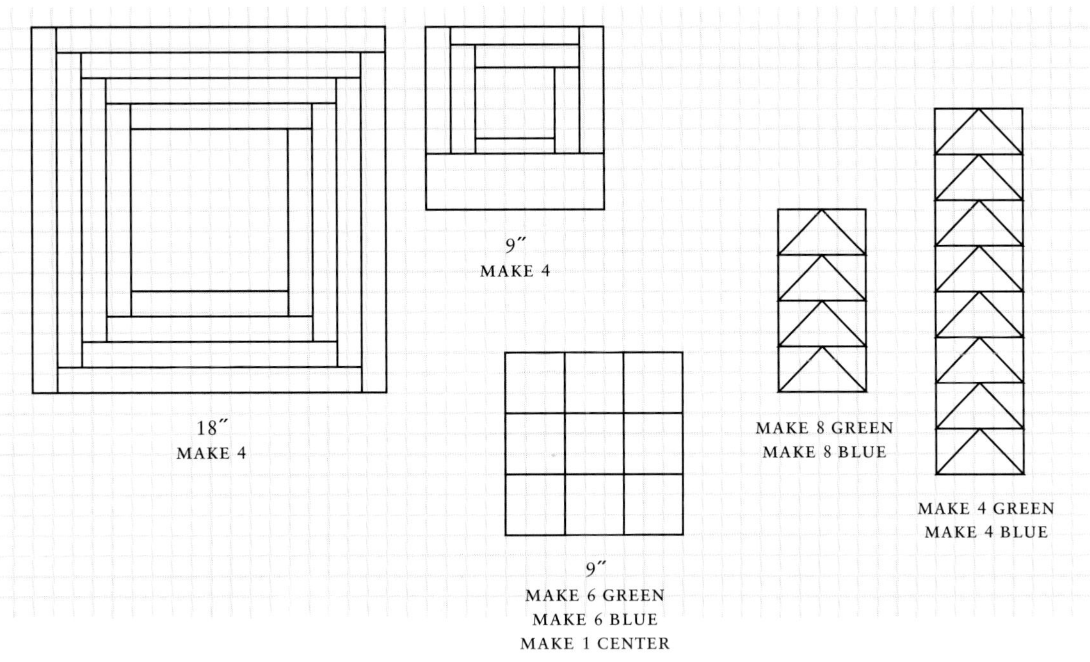

Assembly Diagram

Deneki
Ree Nancarrow and Karla Harris
Collection of Eric A. Nancarrow
74″ x 51″ (189 cm x 130 cm)
Machine pieced, machine quilted, color wash

Deneki

THE MOST EXCITING process in quilt making is using the fabrics in my stash that I love so much. I save some of these fabrics for special projects because I just want to hang on to them forever. Color can make or break a quilt instantly. Color and how you use contrast attract people to a quilt. The ability to see how colors work together is very important in quilt making.

When I begin a new quilt, I like to think design first because it determines what colors I will use. My design is usually based on something pretty realistic. Once an idea forms, I choose the colors next. I start with a small sketch and then enlarge it. If my design has repeating elements, I work up a small piece to see if the whole piece works. It isn't unusual for me to have a stack of fabric three feet tall when I begin pulling fabrics. I love fabric; if one catches my eye, I'll buy it even if I don't need it.

I don't consider trying something different in a quilt taking a risk. I just call it part of the process, and I have never been afraid of ripping out my work.

The thing that motivates me the most to get a quilt done is a deadline. I am still part of the world, and I am not often ready to drop everything so I can work on my quilts nonstop, so sometimes finishing them is tough.

Karla Harris

INSPIRATION

Deneki is the Indian term for moose. After Karla took a watercolor quilt class, she says she "became intrigued with the watercolor process." Talking with her sister, Ree, on the telephone, Karla explained the techniques of a watercolor quilt based on one-and-a-half inch squares. Ree sketched out a moose design and sent it back to Karla. Meanwhile, Karla began cutting out fabric squares, getting ready for a future visit from Ree, when they would jointly make the quilt. Karla's description of the way the sisters work together almost sounds comical; two driven women, working frantically from dawn into all hours of the night, cutting little squares, throwing fabric on the design wall, substituting, making changes, sewing nonstop until the design is complete. This quilt was designed for Eric Nancarrow, Ree's son, as the logo for his business.

TECHNIQUE

Fabric Suggestions and Requirements

Select print fabrics appropriate for color wash quilts. Choose an extremely wide variety of brown, blue, and beige fabrics with a good range of darks to lights. The design will blend and have better transitions if you have a large selection.

Use scraps or buy a large assortment of fabrics in minimum amounts.

1/2 yard (46 cm) for each inside border (pieced)
2 1/2 yards (229 cm) for outside border (unpieced)

Cutting

Cut assorted fabrics into 1 1/2″ (3.8 cm) squares
Cut each inside border 1″ (2.5 cm)
Cut outside border 3 1/2″ (8.9 cm)

Assembly

Draw a 1 1/2″ (3.8 cm) grid on a piece of white flannel that measures 67″ x 44″ (172 cm x 112 cm) for your working wall.

Follow the chart for placement of the sun, moose, and background squares. Rearrange squares until the colors are well blended, giving you the desired effect.

Sew squares into rows, then join rows. Add borders, mitering corners.

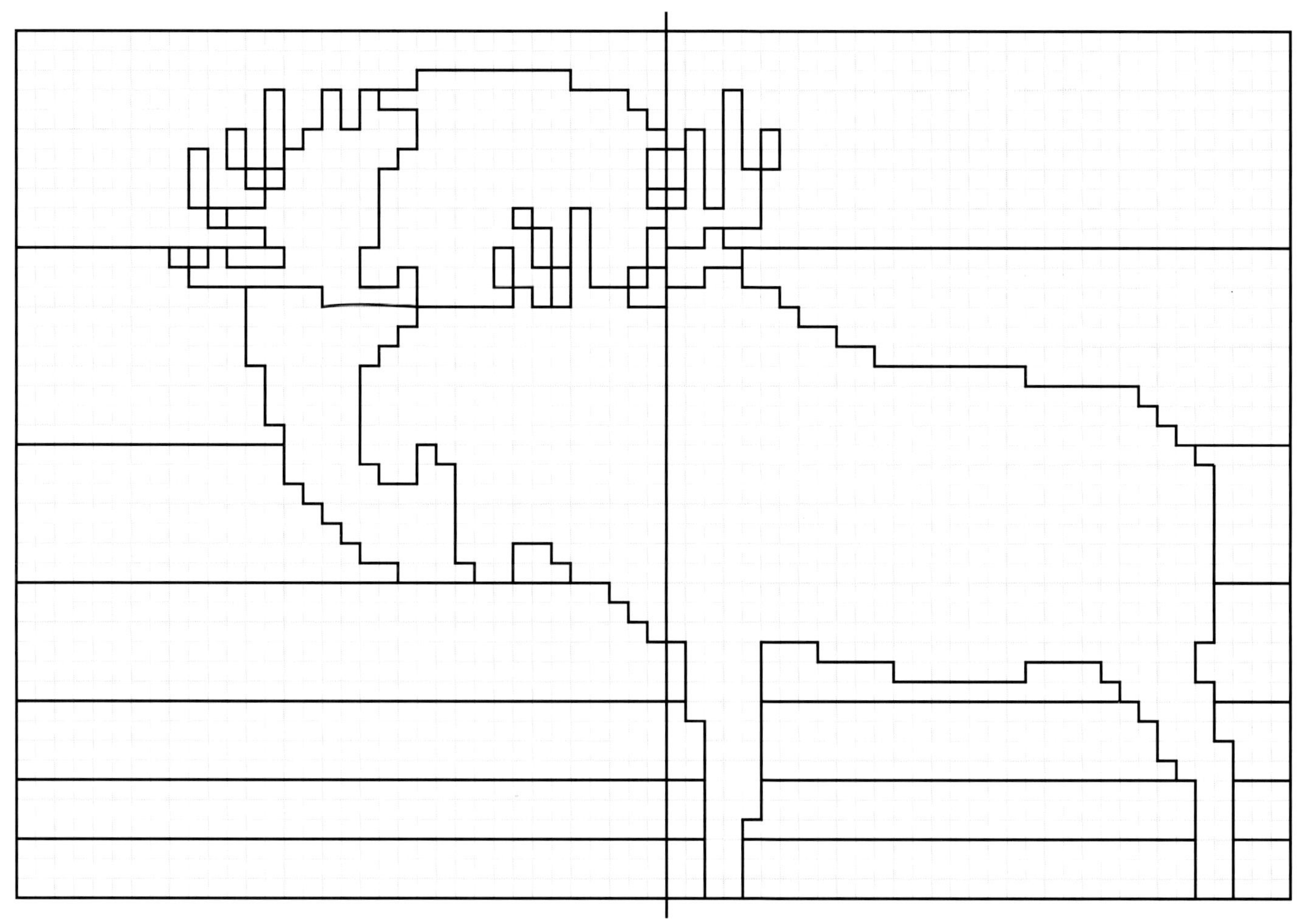

Assembly Diagram

EACH SQUARE EQUALS $1^1/2''$ (3.8 CM)

A Bouquet of Beauties
Joyce R. Becker
Blocks appliquéd by Thursday Group Friends
79″ x 99″ (201 cm x 251 cm) ❧ Hand appliquéd, trapunto, echo and stipple hand quilted

A Bouquet of Beauties

I AM SO PASSIONATE ABOUT quilt making because it deals both with endless creative opportunities and bonding. These factors feed on each other. Quilting offers me a creative outlet, yet it also allows me to have deep, personal friendships with other women who have the same love for this art. The opportunity to vent, share, laugh, and cry with others who are also driven and passionate about their art is as important as the art itself.

Nature quilts attract me because of their intensity of color. When I am outdoors, I often take mental snapshots, looking at the way the light hits something or how many different greens the trees and bushes hold. I store these clips from nature in my brain and use them later in my quilts.

The fabrics I use in my nature quilts reflect the intensities of color in nature. I hand dye many of my fabrics; hand dyeing appeals to me because I like the unexpected results and the surprises. If a particular quilt calls for it, I incorporate a mixture of commercial fabrics and hand-dyed fabrics. Each quilt has it's own requirements.

Joyce R. Becker

INSPIRATION

I have always loved the iris flower. When I moved to the Northwest, I fell in love with the iris all over again. Everywhere I looked, irises grew in colors I had never seen before, ranging from almost black to azure blue and regal purple. I knew that one day I would have to make an iris quilt. When the opportunity came knocking in the form of friendship blocks with my "Thursday Group" quilting friends, I took it. The long title of this quilt is A Bouquet of Bellyaching Beauties by my Thursday Friends because they gave me endless grief that I had the nerve to choose an appliqué block instead of a pieced block and then made them select predetermined colors. However, after their blocks were done, most of my friends secretly told me they were glad I forced them into trying appliqué and that they now love it! My extreme gratitude to: Rosy Carolan, Melody Crust, Patti Cunningham, Denise Good, Yvonne Grobe, Marian Holste, Connie James, Ruthann Lindsay, Shirley Meredith, Pat Michelsen, Candy Stover, Debbie White and Patti Yasue.

TECHNIQUE

14˝ x 14˝ (35.6 cm x 35.6 cm) block

Fabric Suggestions

Select colors of your choice for iris petals and stems.

1/4 yard (23 cm) for petals in one iris block
1/4 yard (23 cm) for stems in one iris block
10 yards (914 cm) quality muslin for background
Floral fabric for bias and binding, if desired

Cutting

Cut 31—14 1/2˝ (36.8 cm) background squares for blocks

Cut 5—22˝ (55.9 cm) squares; cutting diagonally twice for 18 side triangles

Cut the required number of petals and stems from templates

Instructions

Appliqué pieces to muslin in numerical order, using diagram 1 as your guide. Embellish some of the appliquéd blocks with French knots. Draft and appliqué small butterflies, if desired. Sew blocks and triangles together in rows as shown in diagram 2. Sew rows together to complete the quilt top.

Quilting and Embellishments

If you wish to use trapunto on the center block, you must stuff the block before quilting. Trace the iris template pattern onto the center block, then use your favorite method of stuffing. Refer to *Step by Step Trapunto and Stippling* in Resources.

This piece is heavily quilted. If you choose to do stippling in the center, it is necessary to continue heavy quilting throughout the piece so it will hang straight. Stipple quilt in a herringbone pattern around each iris. Echo quilt around iris block in 1/8˝ (3 mm) increments.

Draft a feather design of your choice and transfer it to your quilt top, using the photo as your reference. Make 1/2˝ (13 mm) wide bias in a floral fabric to use as your feather spine. Appliqué spine onto feather design. If desired, use a double row of quilting in the feather. Use a light green quilting thread for accent. Quilt remainder of top with horizontal lines, using 1/4˝ masking tape for guidance. Fill in every other 1/4˝ (6 mm) space with an additional quilting line. Bind with same fabric used in feather spine.

Diagram 1
Appliqué Block

Diagram 2

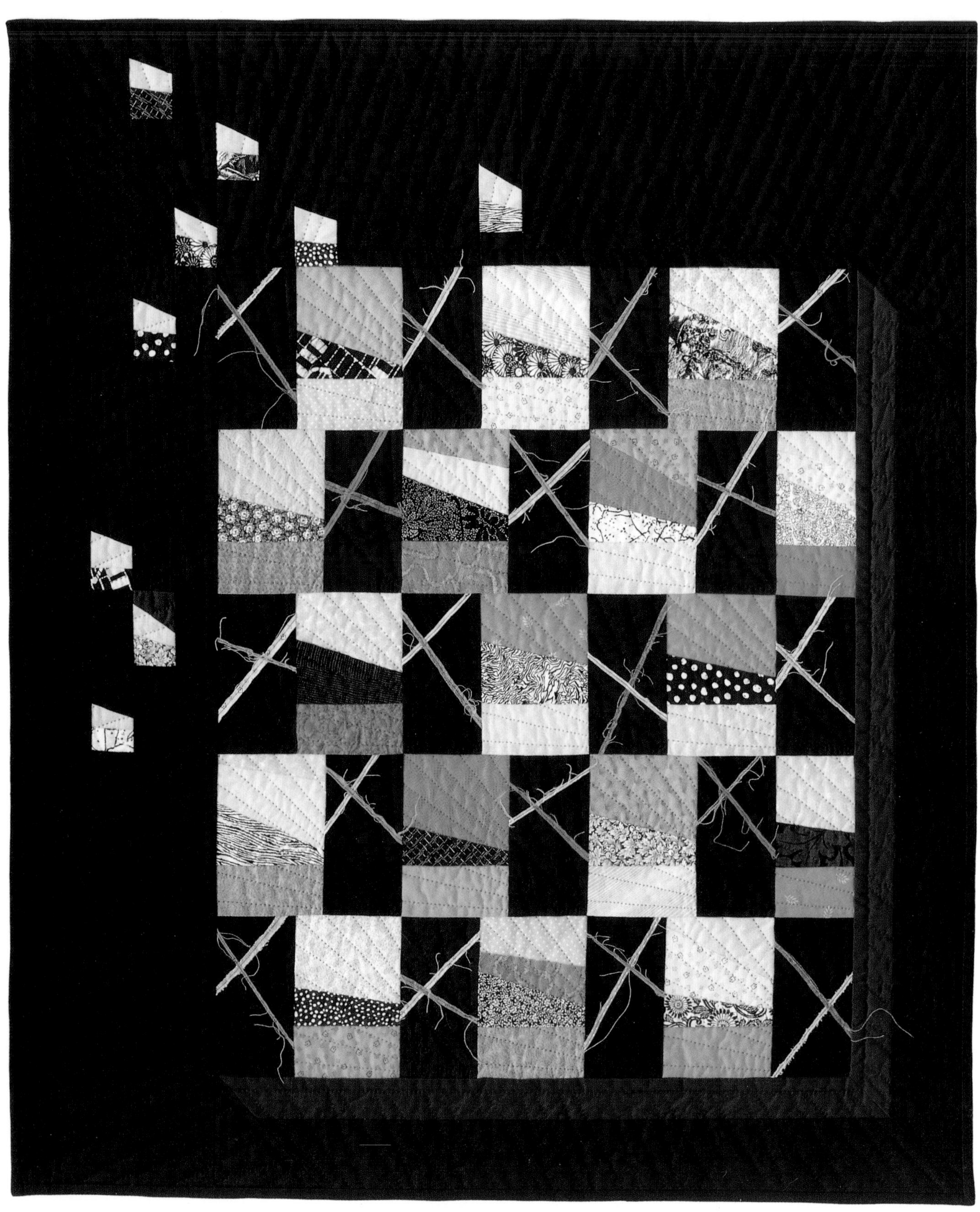

Goldfinches at the Feeder
Heather W. Tewell
33″ x 40″ (84 cm x 102 cm)
Machine pieced and appliquéd, hand quilted

Goldfinches at the Feeder

CREATING ART is a tremendously difficult process. You can know all of the supposed rules about the process of quilt making, but you have to study and look at each piece as it is being created. I'm rarely happy with the first idea that comes to mind, and I have to go away from it and let my subconscious work. That's part of my creative process and I cannot afford to be impatient.

I tend to create designs as I go along, so I need big chunks of time for playing around with ideas for my quilts. It's like my motor starts going and needs to keep running for a while in order for the really good ideas to come. When my mind is in gear and in tune with the quilt, creativity follows.

I try to keep my mind open for possibilities. I never graph or draw out my designs. I might make a rough sketch but generally I design my quilts in my head. When I am working on a particular quilt, I try to have a full color palette on hand before I start. Then I challenge myself to use only what I have on hand for my finished project.

Quilting is such an integral part of my life. Each quilt offers something new—new colors, new techniques, and new choices. I used to make quilts just for myself, but that has changed. I want my quilts to be more unique and original, and I hope my audience responds to what I try to accomplish with each piece.

Heather W Tewell

INSPIRATION

Shut your eyes tightly and envision the following scene. It is a typical Northwest day: The skies are gray, and the water is lapping gently against the shore of Puget Sound. As you look out your window, you notice the bird feeder is loaded with the most gorgeous array of goldfinches you have ever seen. The intense gold next to the stark black of their feathers, playing against the orange of their beaks and the spontaneous mixing of white immediately triggers an idea for your next quilt. Why not create a quilt depicting birds feeding? The goldfinches would then be startled by movement, the fluttering of their wings shown as offset blocks made with shredded strips. Heather's whimsical interpretation of this vision was captured near her Puget Sound beach "getaway" home, in Anacortes, Washington.

TECHNIQUE

Fabric Requirements

3/4 yard (69 cm) assorted yellow prints
1/2 yard (46 cm) assorted black prints
1 1/4 yards (114 cm) solid black

Instructions

A is strip pieced. Cut 5″ strips from yellow prints. Cut 5″ strips from black prints. Cut 2 1/4″ strips from yellow prints. Make 17 A's following diagram 1. Trim each to 4 1/4″ x 6″ (10.8 cm x 15.2 cm).

B is also strip pieced. Cut 2″ strips from solid black. Cut 2″ strips from yellow prints. Cut 1 1/2″ strips from black prints. Make 9 B's following diagram 1. Trim each to 2″ x 3 1/2″ (5.1 cm x 8.9 cm).

C	Cut 4	2″ x 3 1/2″ (5.1 cm x 8.9 cm)
D	Cut 2	3 1/2″ square (8.9 cm)
E	Cut 2	3 1/4″ x 3 1/2″ (8.3 cm x 8.9 cm)
F	Cut 2	2″ x 5 1/2″ (5.1 cm x 14.0 cm)
G	Cut 1	12″ x 8 1/2″ (30.5 cm x 21 cm)
H	Cut 1	5 1/2″ x 6 1/2″ (14.0 cm x 16 cm)
I	Cut 1	2 1/2″ x 11 1/4″ (6.4 cm x 28.6 cm)
J	Cut 1	4″ x 11 1/2″ (10.2 cm x 29.2 cm)
K	Cut 1	5″ square (12.7 cm)
L	Cut 1	2 1/2″ x 14″ (5.7 cm x 35.6 cm)
M	Cut 1	7″ x 16″ (17.8 cm x 40 cm)
X	Cut 18	3 1/4″ x 6″ (8.2 cm x 15.2 cm)

The A, B, and X blocks are strip pieced blocks made by sewing consecutive strips to a base strip, then trimming blocks to exact measurements.

Make the A blocks beginning with a base strip of 2 1/4″ (5.6 cm). Sew one strip to the base strip, right sides together. Press. Place the next strip on top, right side up, and trim both at an angle. Turn the strip over and sew the angled strip onto the unit. Trim each block to 4 1/4″ x 6″ (10.8 cm x 15.2 cm). See diagram 1.

Make the B blocks in the same way beginning with a base strip of 1 1/2″ (3.8 cm). Trim each block 2″ x 3 1/2″ (5.1 cm x 8.9 cm).

Make the X blocks by sewing very narrow yellow strips of fabric in random "X" patterns to the solid black 3 1/4″ x 6″ (8.3 cm x 15.2 cm) rectangles.

Assembly

Assemble the quilt top in units, using diagram 2 as a guide. Sew Blocks A and X in rows as shown, trimming Block A in rows 2 and 4 where necessary. Sew the upper section to the block section. Attach borders and triangles. Miter the corners of the border. Sew the side section together in groups. Sew completed side section to quilt top.

Quilting

Machine or hand quilt, using the photo as a guide.

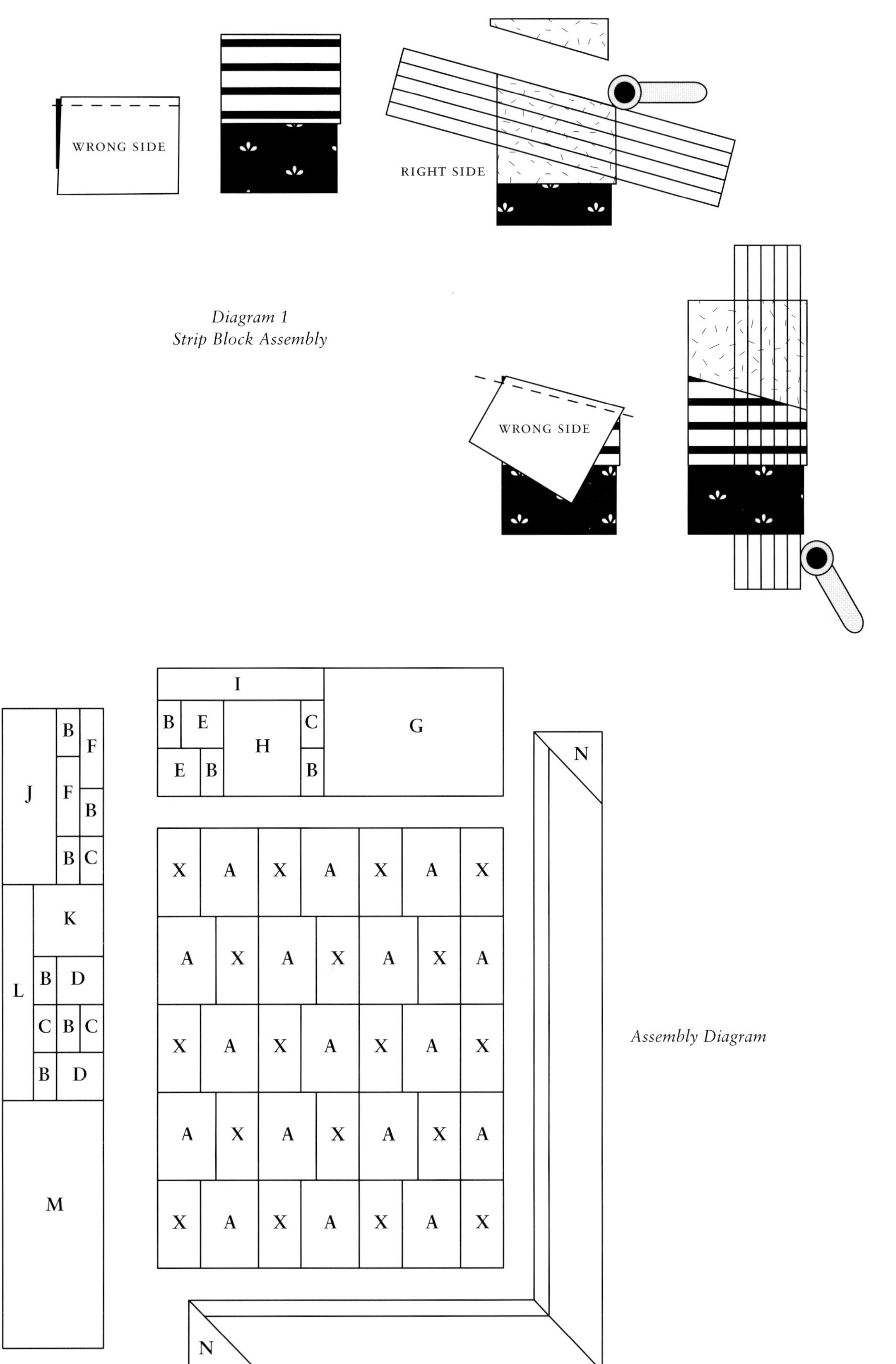

Diagram 1
Strip Block Assembly

Assembly Diagram

Mostly Lichens
Jane Herbst
44″ x 40″ (112 cm x 102 cm)
Machine embroidered and appliquéd, machine pieced and quilted

Mostly Lichens

THE CHALLENGE in my work is to incorporate as much detail and realism as possible. My work is a natural science lesson wrapped up in a piece of art. The emphasis is on creations that people are not familiar with. Each piece of art is in a different embryonic stage in my brain, and when each one is born, then I go to paper with it. I'll draw my idea to make sure the proportions are right and my idea works. Then I lay out my backing material, which is like a stiff canvas fabric, and I iron on a stabilizer, which makes it even stiffer. At this point, I sketch out with a pencil where my main design elements go on the background material. Then, I cut bits of fabric that will be the background. I do a section at a time, doing the background first then the machine embroidery, working my way around until the whole thing is finished. At this point, I'll look at the piece for a few days. If I am satisfied with it, I will begin machine quilting.

There is some evidence that the popularity of quilt art is growing in acceptance and I hope there will come a time when this medium is recognized as a serious art form. I see the work I do as multi-leveled and feel it appeals to different people on different levels. Someone who knows nothing about the medium might look at the colors and shapes and say, "How in the world did she do that," while a fiber artist might appreciate the techniques used.

Jane Herbst

INSPIRATION

The first time I saw Mostly Lichens, I immediately wanted to touch and feel it. It seemed that the embroidered shapes depicting the undergrowth were alive because they looked so realistic. I stared at it, transfixed for the longest time, almost feeling like I was a part of this environment that Jane says "epitomizes the symbiotic lifestyle of the many lichens, mushrooms, and rattlesnake orchids." I wondered what kind of scientific and artistic background the artist had in order to present such detailed, precise interpretations.

Once I spoke with Jane and discovered she had training as a scientific illustrator who dabbled with watercolors on the side, I breathed a sigh of relief and felt better. To me, Jane's description of her work as "illustrations using thread and fabric" is profound. She says her pieces aren't quilts, rather "three layers quilted together using thread and fiber as the medium." She has created her own artistic niche.

Epilogue

WHAT A JOURNEY this has been! I've enjoyed the wide diversity of concepts, inspirations, and emotions that have come from the contributing artists. At times, when interviewing them, I found myself almost chuckling. Their responses were often totally opposite, depending on the artist. I learned that when it comes to quilt art, there are no wrongs and there are no rights. Your quilt art is personal. If you perceive it to be quilt art, then it is. This medium offers each of us the opportunity to freeze mental images based in nature and create our own original, unique interpretations.

Perhaps certain words from the artists' profiles jumped off the page to grab your attention and give you a little jolt of electricity. I thought it would be nice to share some things with you that I found particularly insightful, that provoked new thoughts and directions in me. "If a quilt is forced, it doesn't work; it has to jell," really struck a nerve. How many times have you plodded on with a quilt even though it wasn't working? Putting it "away to bake," seemed to me to be a very logical solution.

Deep emotions tied to quilting ran the gambit in my interviews. Words like: justification, intuition, impulse, capture a moment, follow your heart, optimism, tactile, calming, self-expression, validation, escape, respite, satisfying, spontaneous, joy, whimsical, creative and fun seemed to ooze from the artists with such depth and sincerity that I was truly moved.

Writing this closing paragraph almost brings tears to my eyes. I have grown so much as a result of this adventure that I hate for it to end. I find myself looking at nature with fresh eyes, and I see a bounty of possibilities for my art in the future. I hope you, too, will consider veering off the "safe path" and realize your potential for discovery and self-expression.

Templates

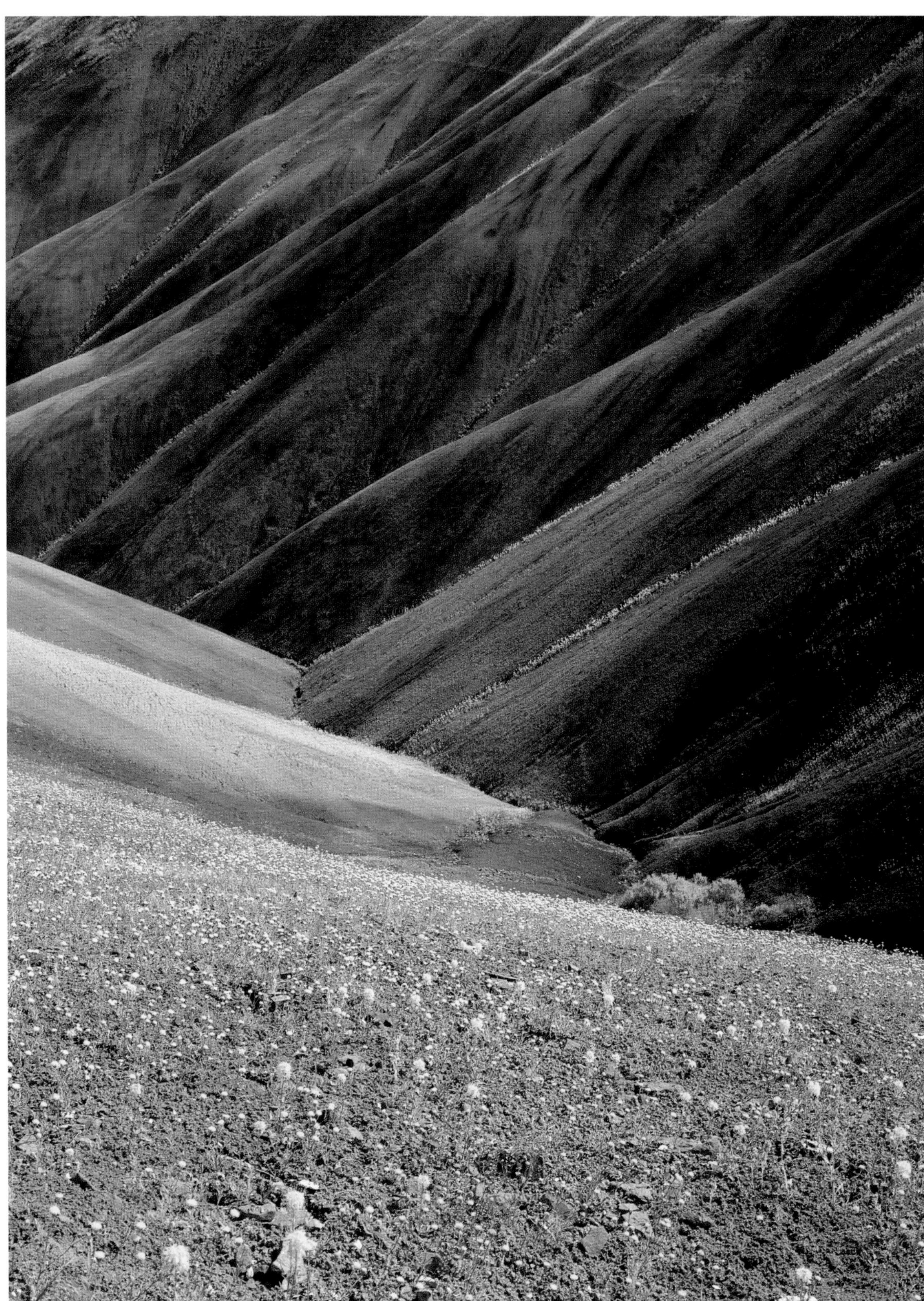

John Day Chaenactis flowers on colored slopes, painted Hills, J.D. Fossil Beds National Monument, OR.

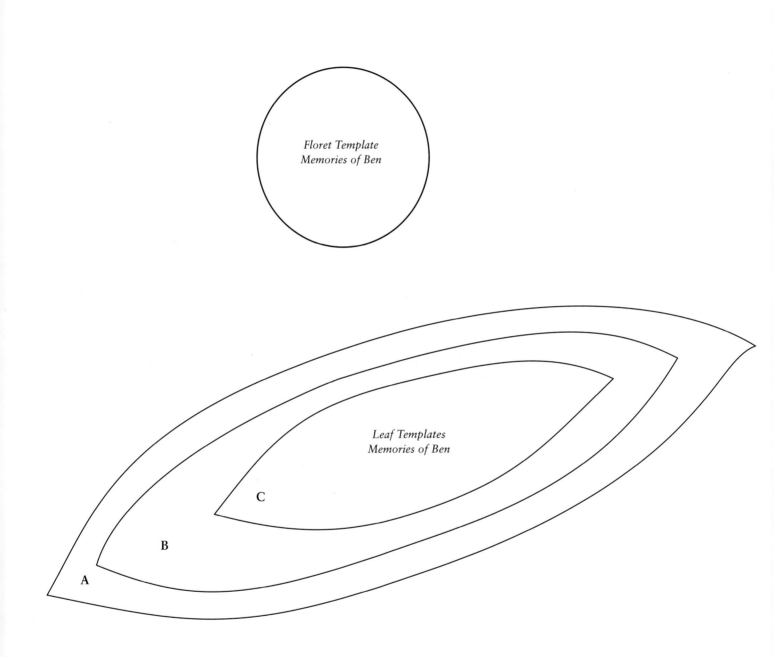

Floret Template
Memories of Ben

Leaf Templates
Memories of Ben

C

B

A

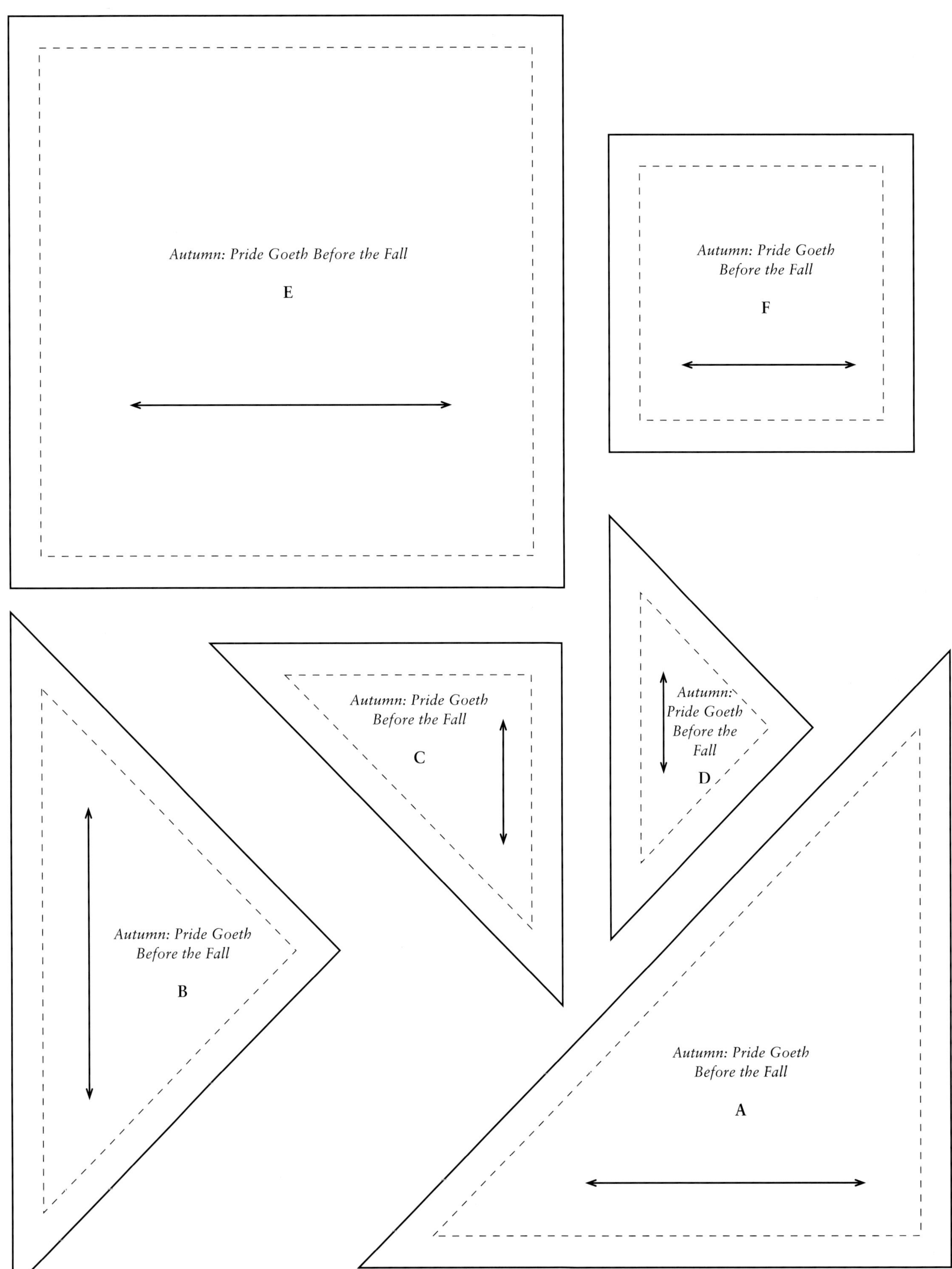
Autumn: Pride Goeth Before the Fall
E
Autumn: Pride Goeth
Before the Fall
F
Autumn: Pride Goeth
Before the Fall
C
Autumn:
Pride Goeth
Before the
Fall
D
Autumn: Pride Goeth
Before the Fall
B
Autumn: Pride Goeth
Before the Fall
A

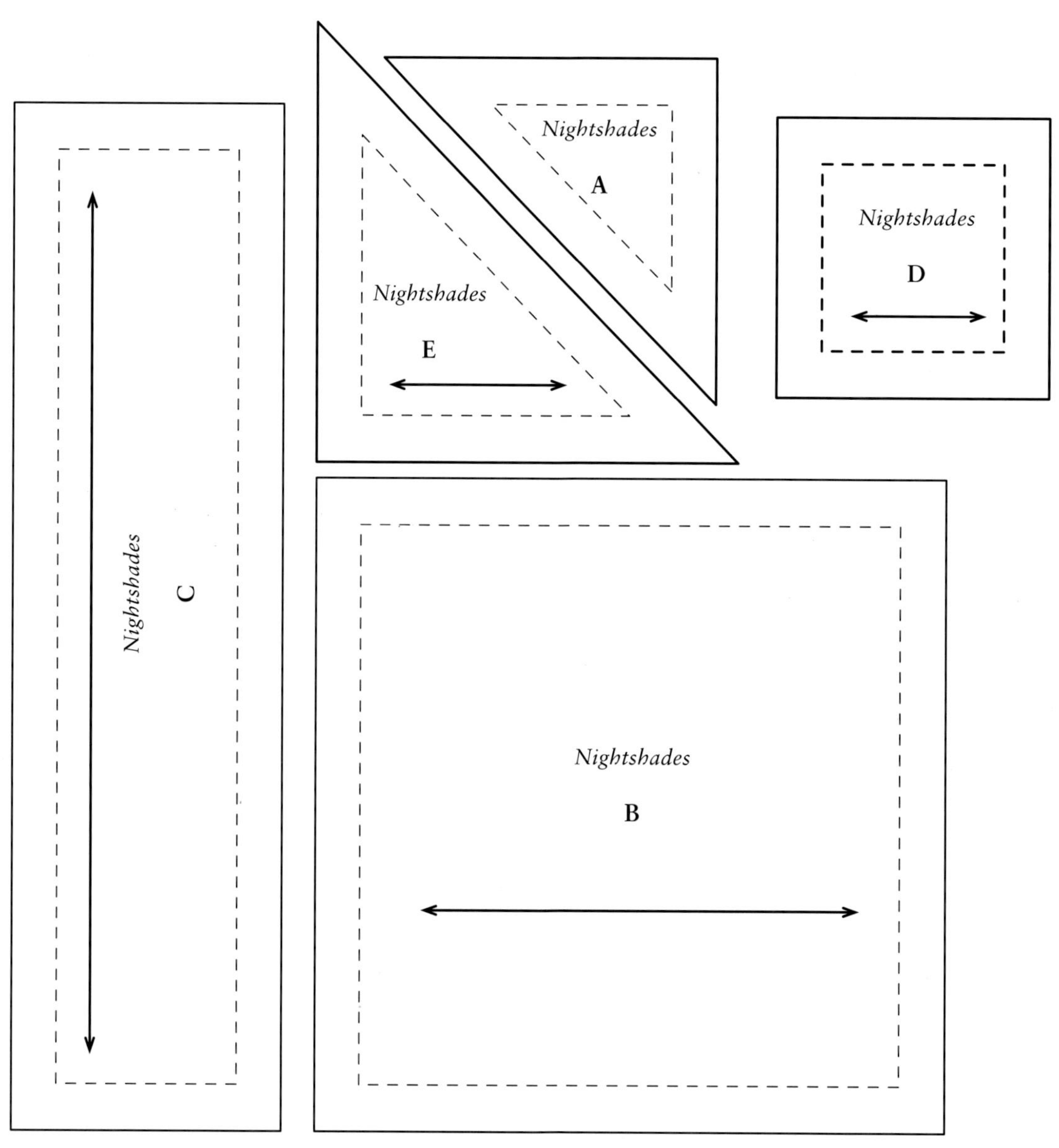
Nightshades
A
Nightshades
E
Nightshades
D
Nightshades
C
Nightshades
B

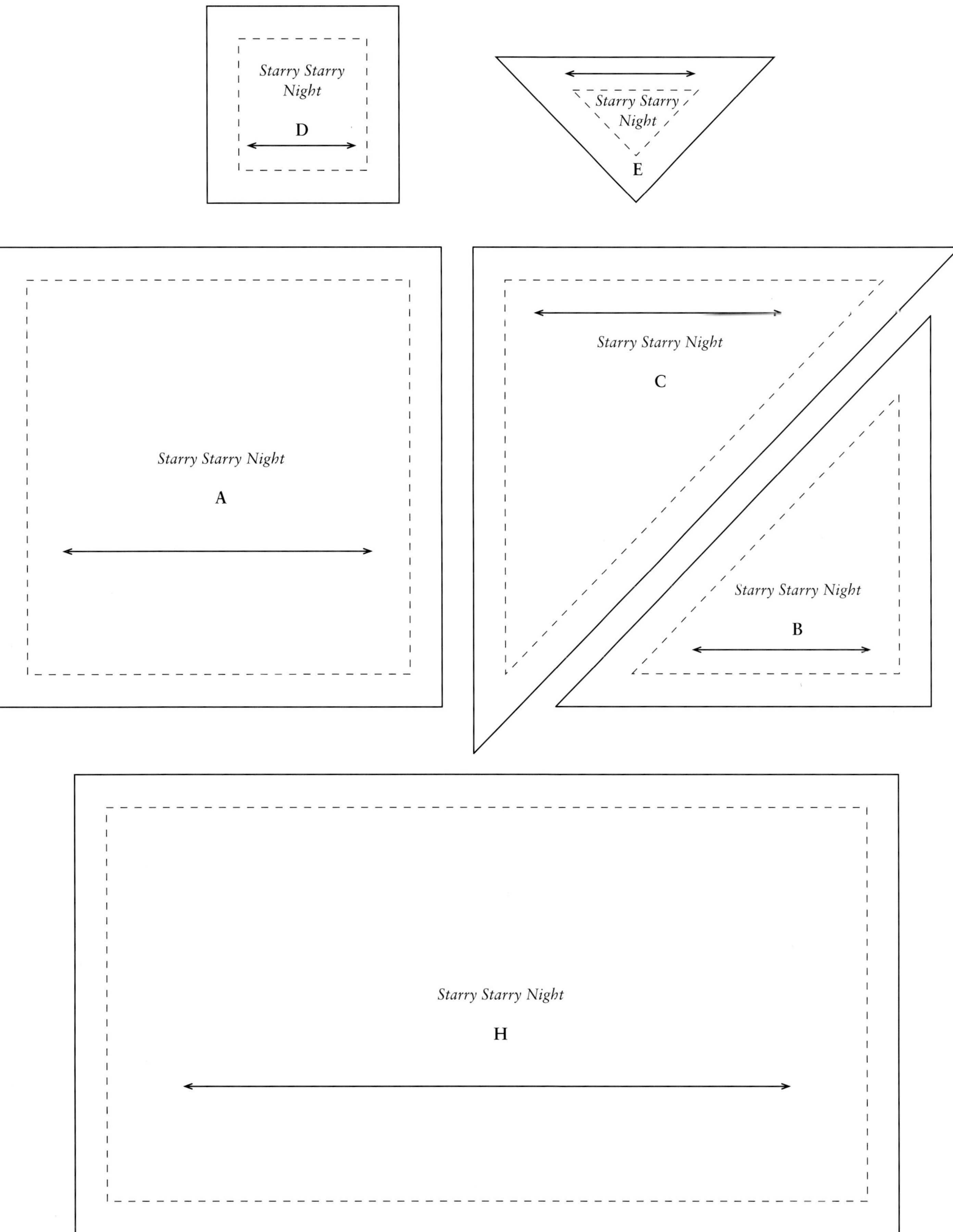
Starry Starry Night
D
Starry Starry Night
E
Starry Starry Night
A
Starry Starry Night
C
Starry Starry Night
B
Starry Starry Night
H

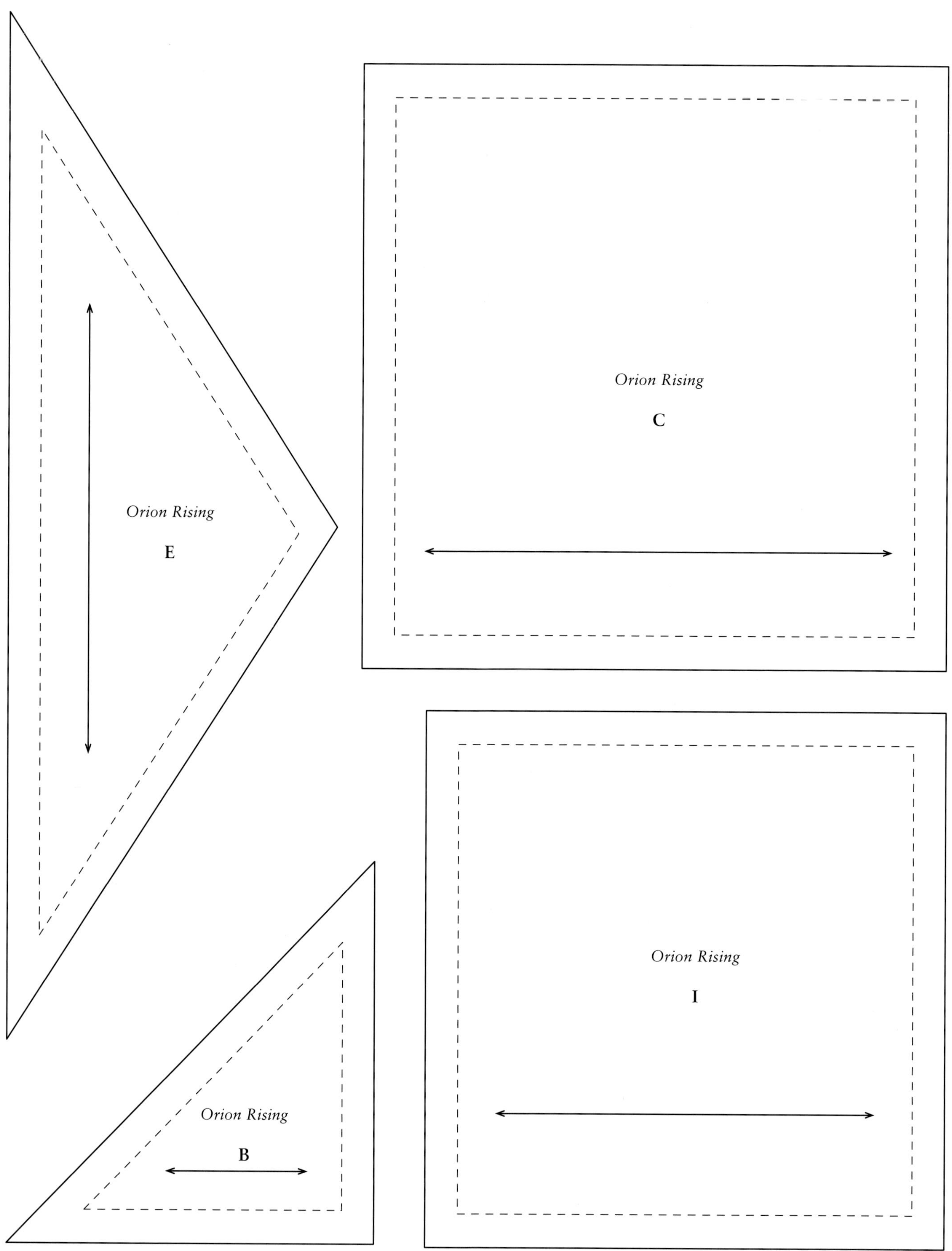
Orion Rising
E
Orion Rising
C
Orion Rising
I
Orion Rising
B

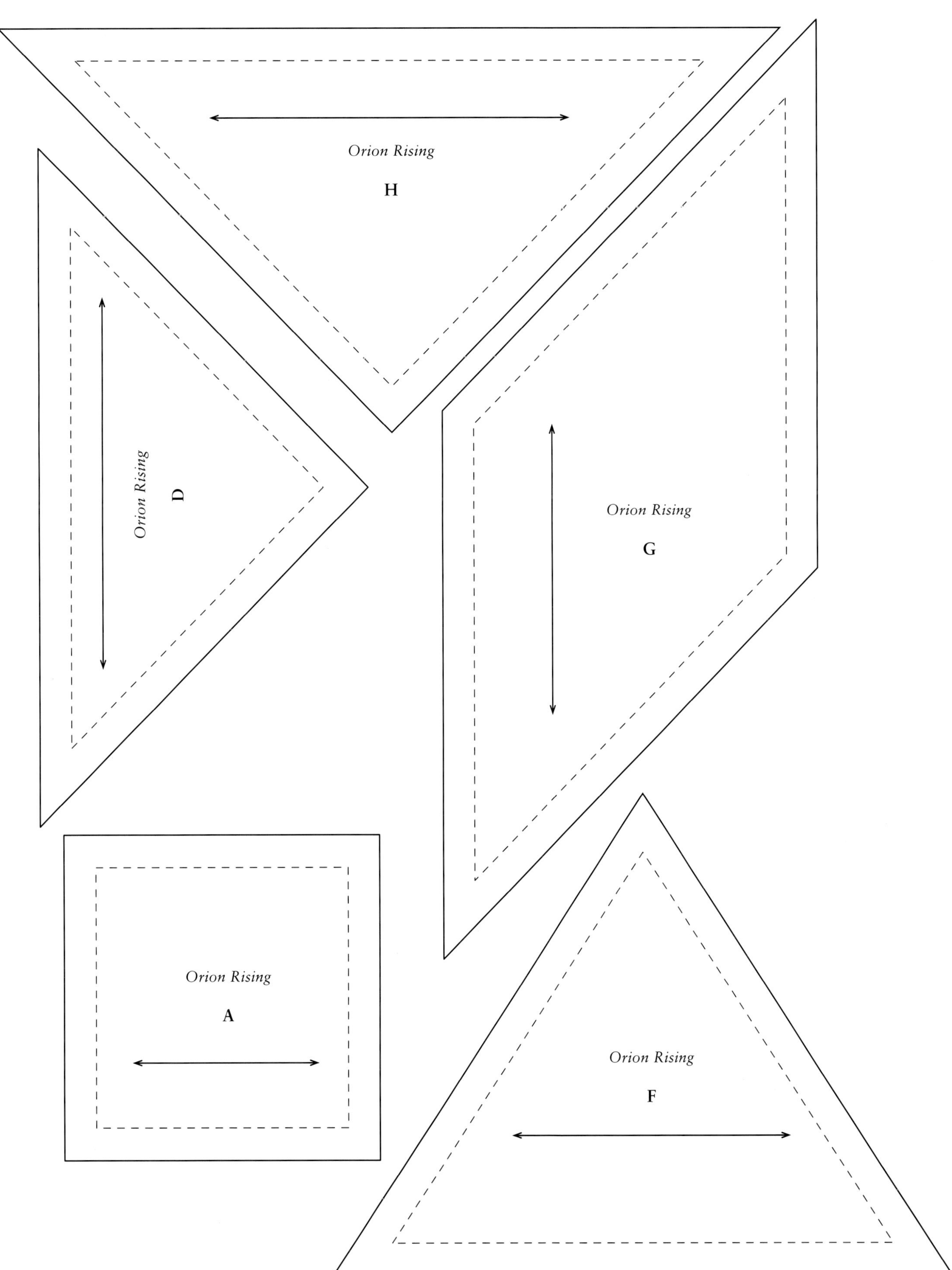
Orion Rising
H
Orion Rising
D
Orion Rising
G
Orion Rising
A
Orion Rising
F

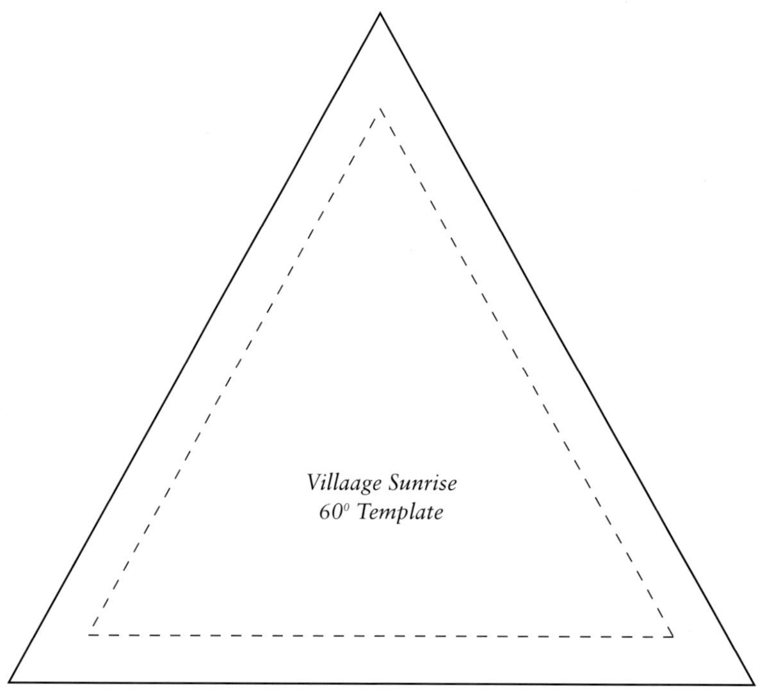
Villaage Sunrise
60° Template

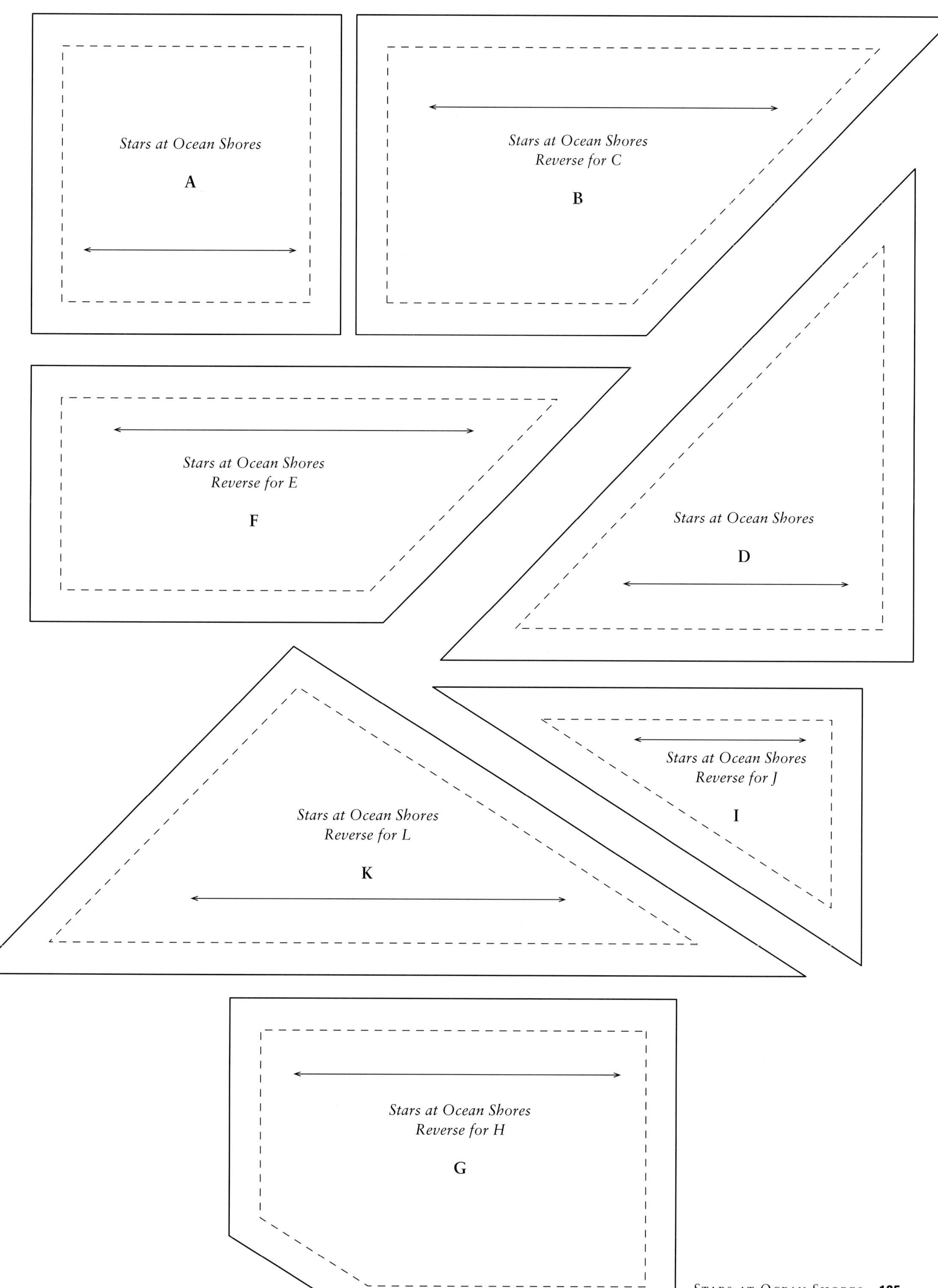
Stars at Ocean Shores
A
Stars at Ocean Shores
Reverse for C
B
Stars at Ocean Shores
Reverse for E
F
Stars at Ocean Shores
D
Stars at Ocean Shores
Reverse for J
I
Stars at Ocean Shores
Reverse for L
K
Stars at Ocean Shores
Reverse for H
G

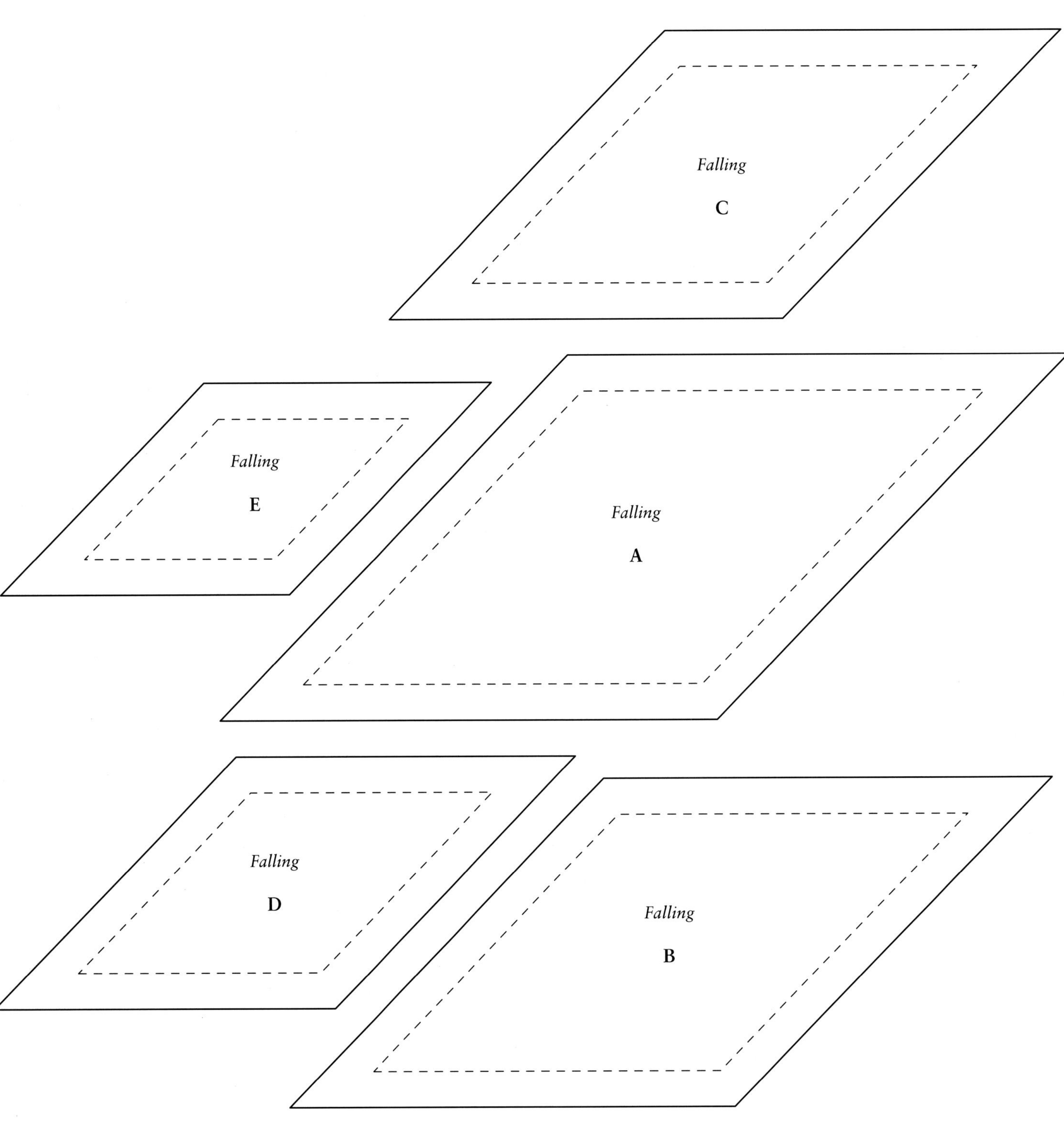
Falling
C
Falling
E
Falling
A
Falling
D
Falling
B

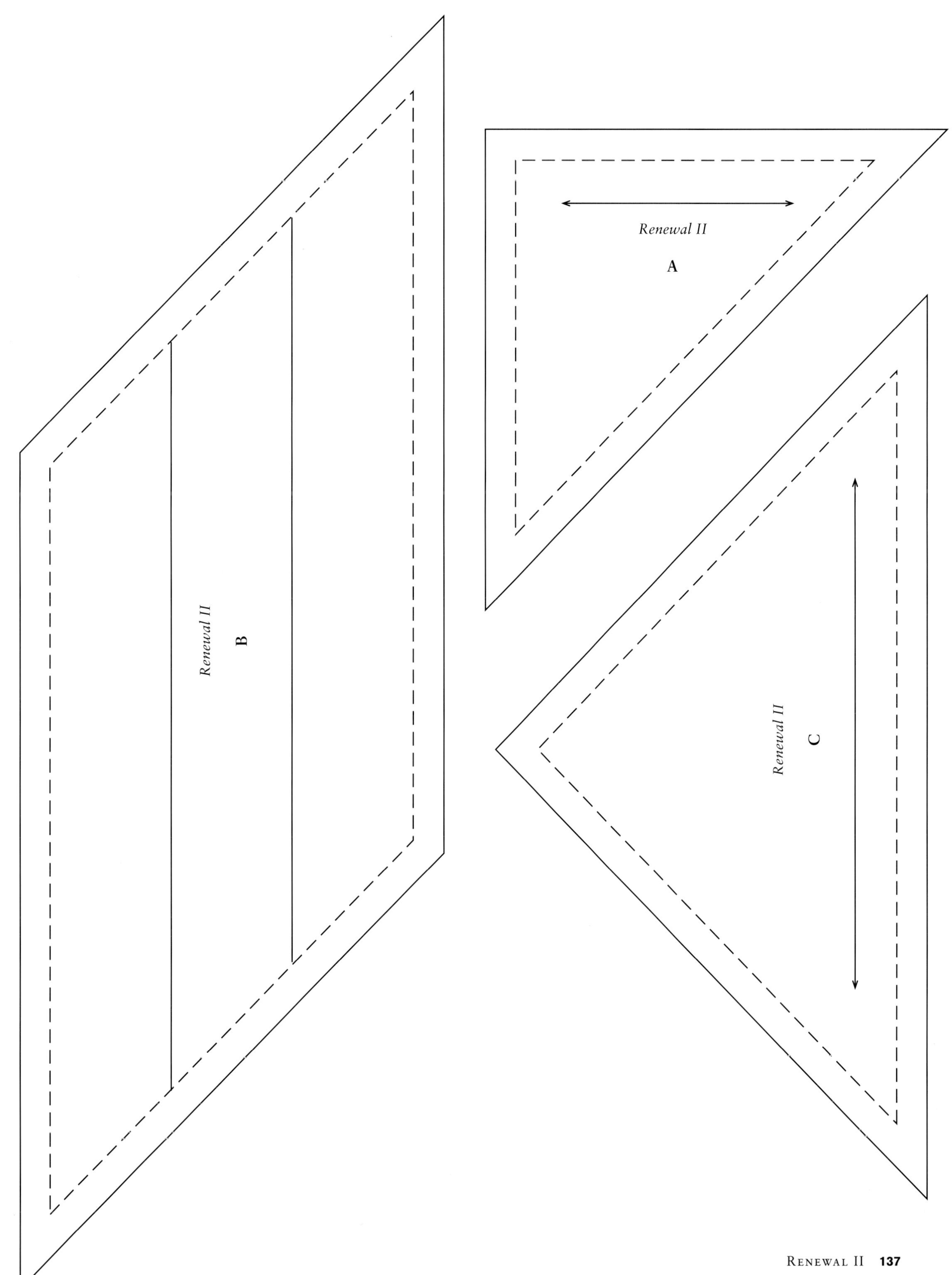
Renewal II
A
Renewal II
B
Renewal II
C

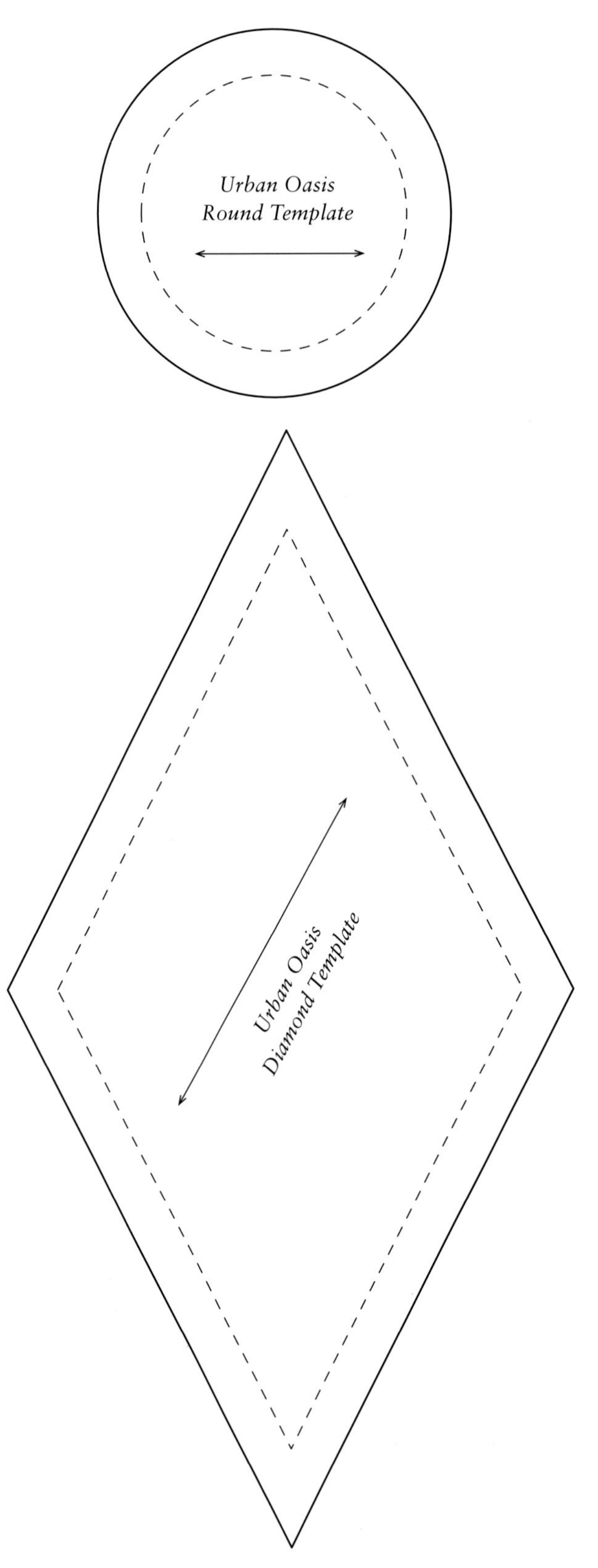
Urban Oasis
Round Template
Urban Oasis
Diamond Template

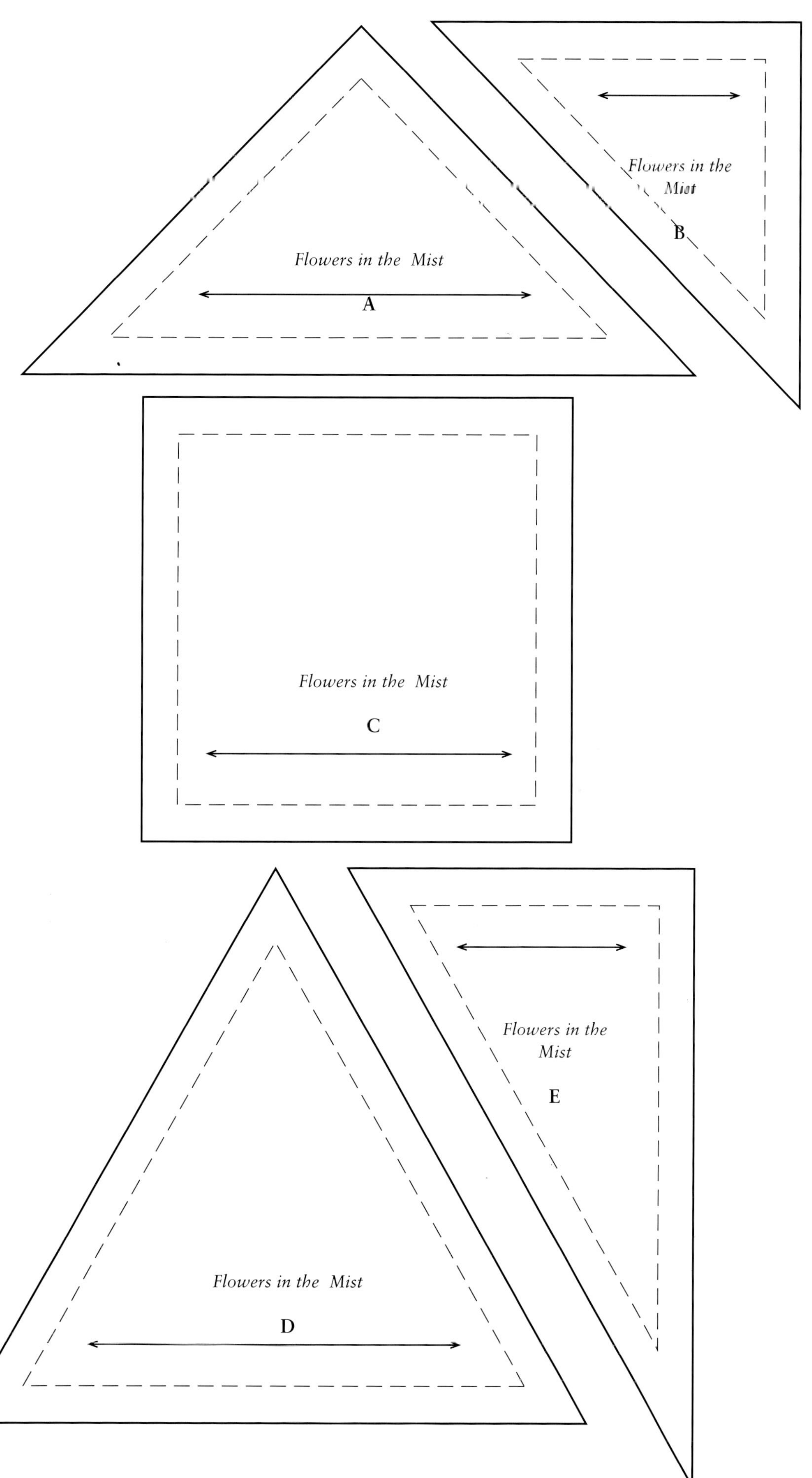
Flowers in the Mist
A
Flowers in the Mist
B
Flowers in the Mist
C
Flowers in the Mist
D
Flowers in the Mist
E

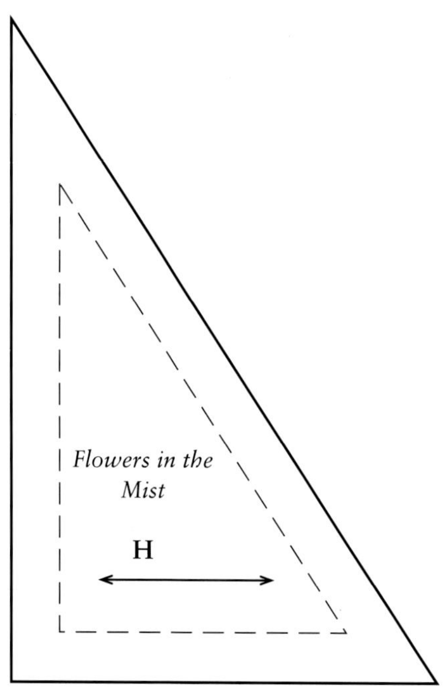
Flowers in the
Mist
H

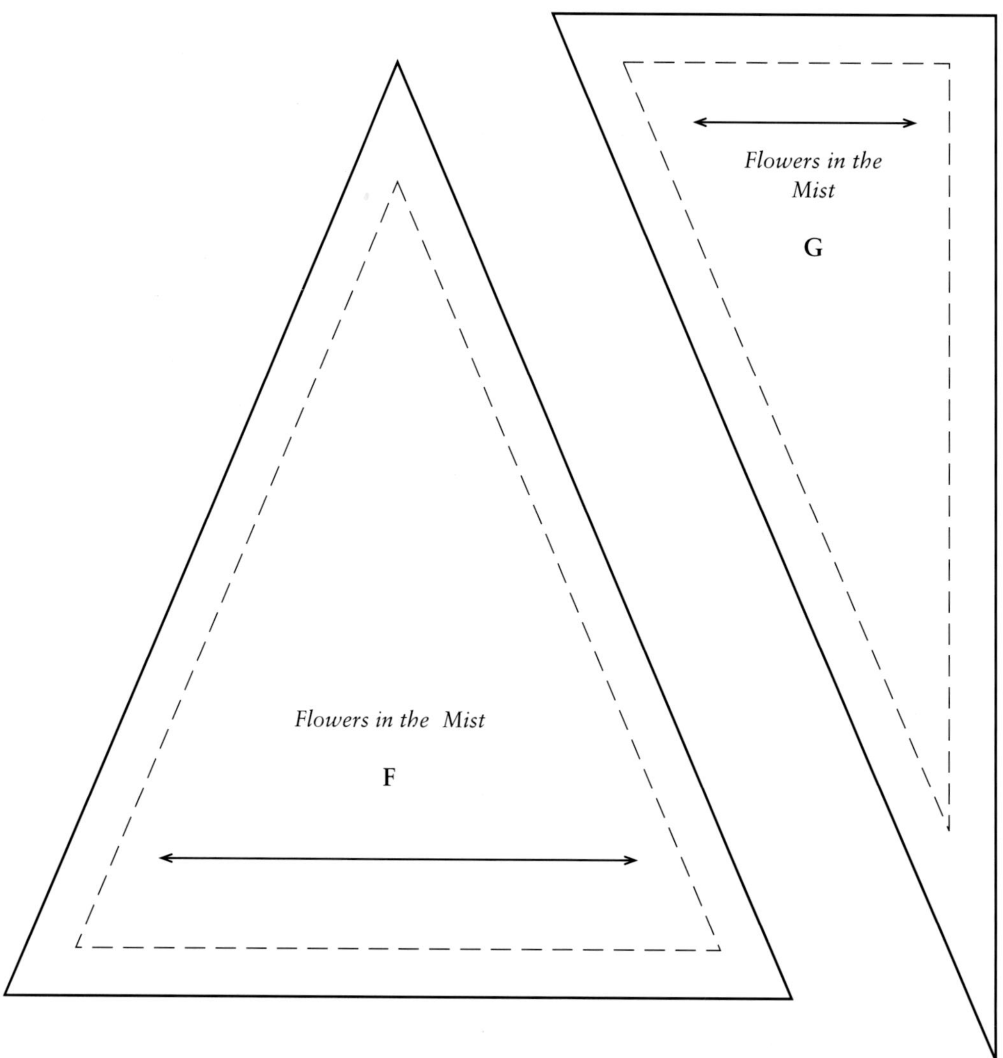
Flowers in the
Mist
G
Flowers in the Mist
F

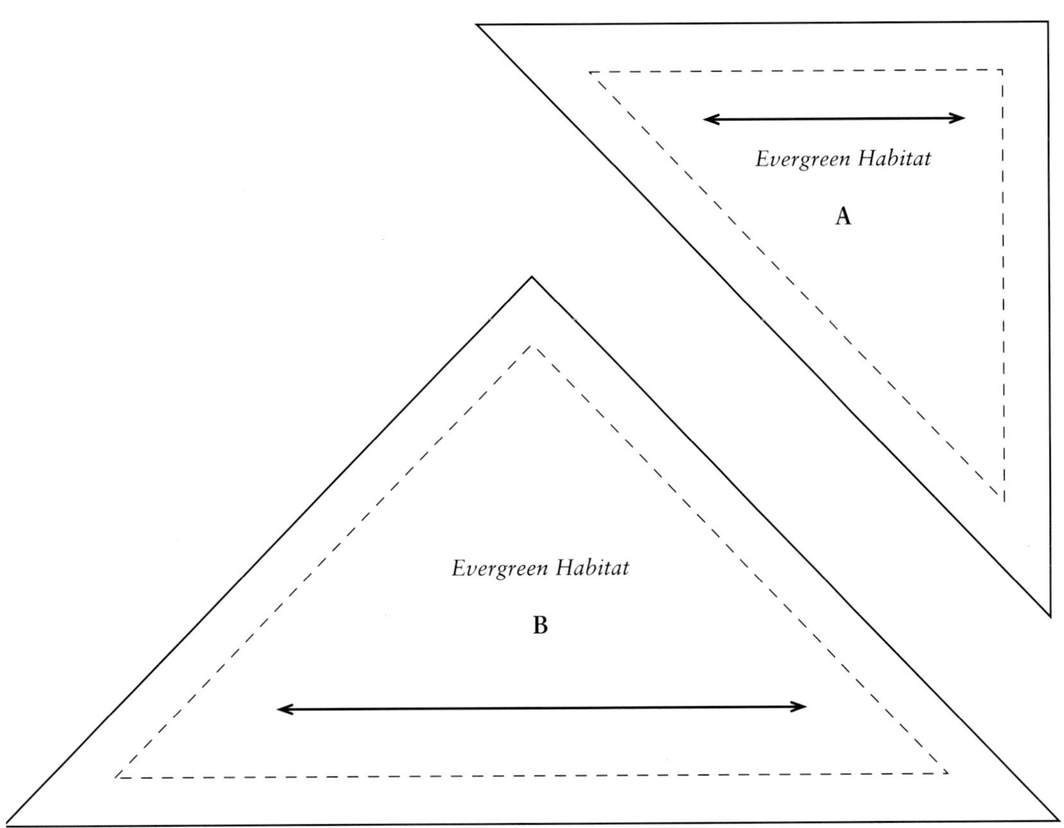
Evergreen Habitat
A
Evergreen Habitat
B

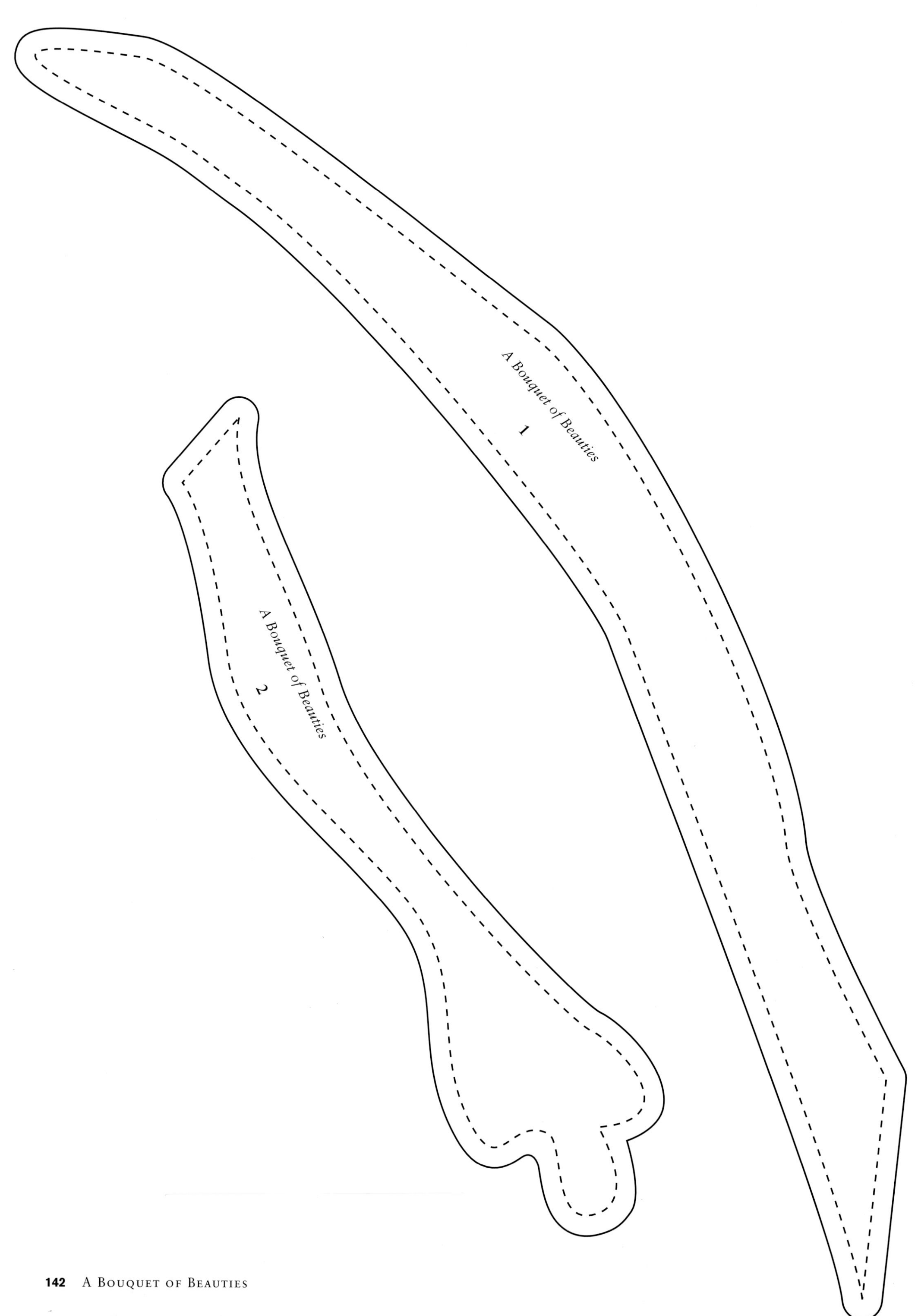
A Bouquet of Beauties
1
A Bouquet of Beauties
2

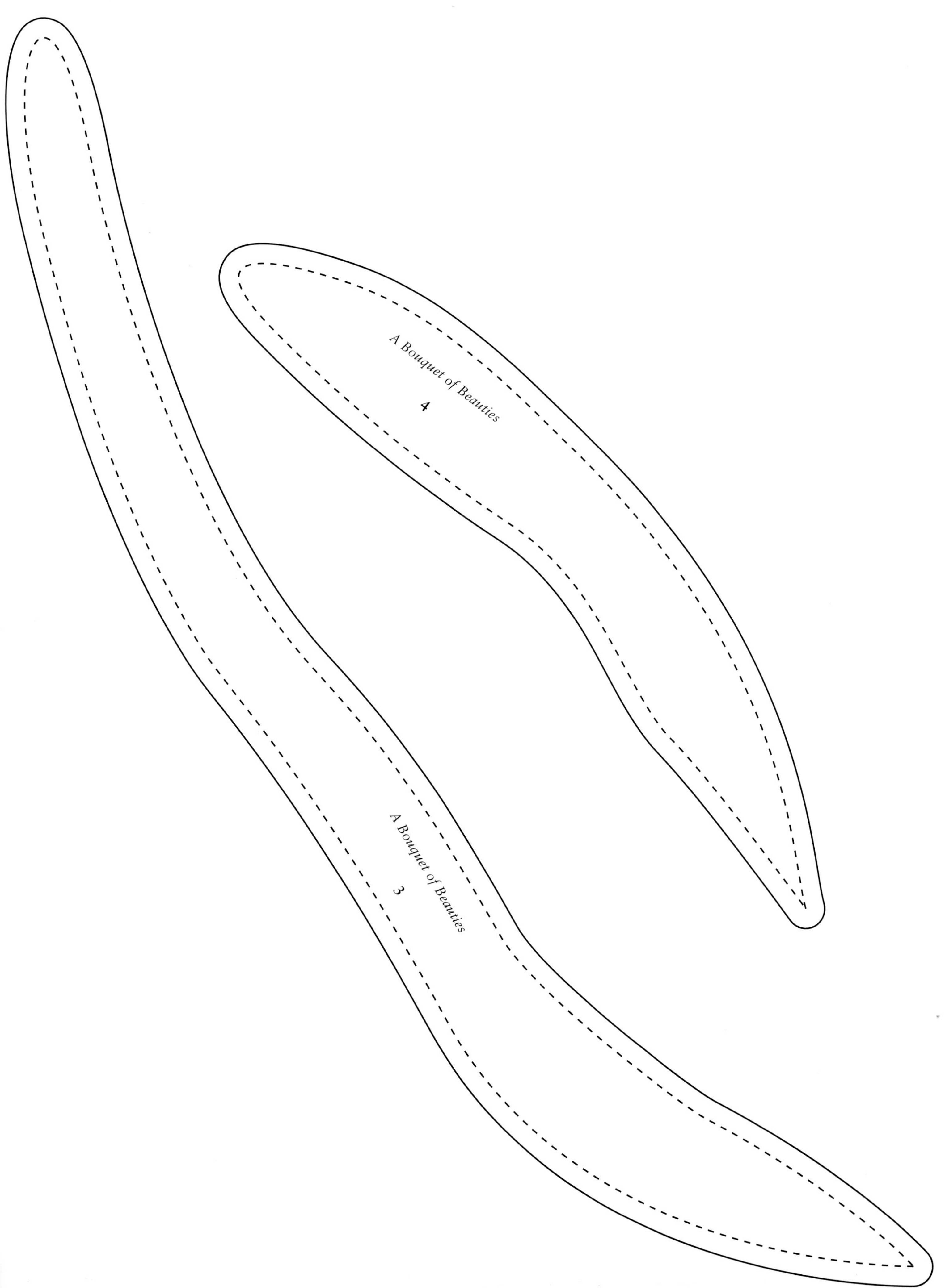
A Bouquet of Beauties
4
A Bouquet of Beauties
3

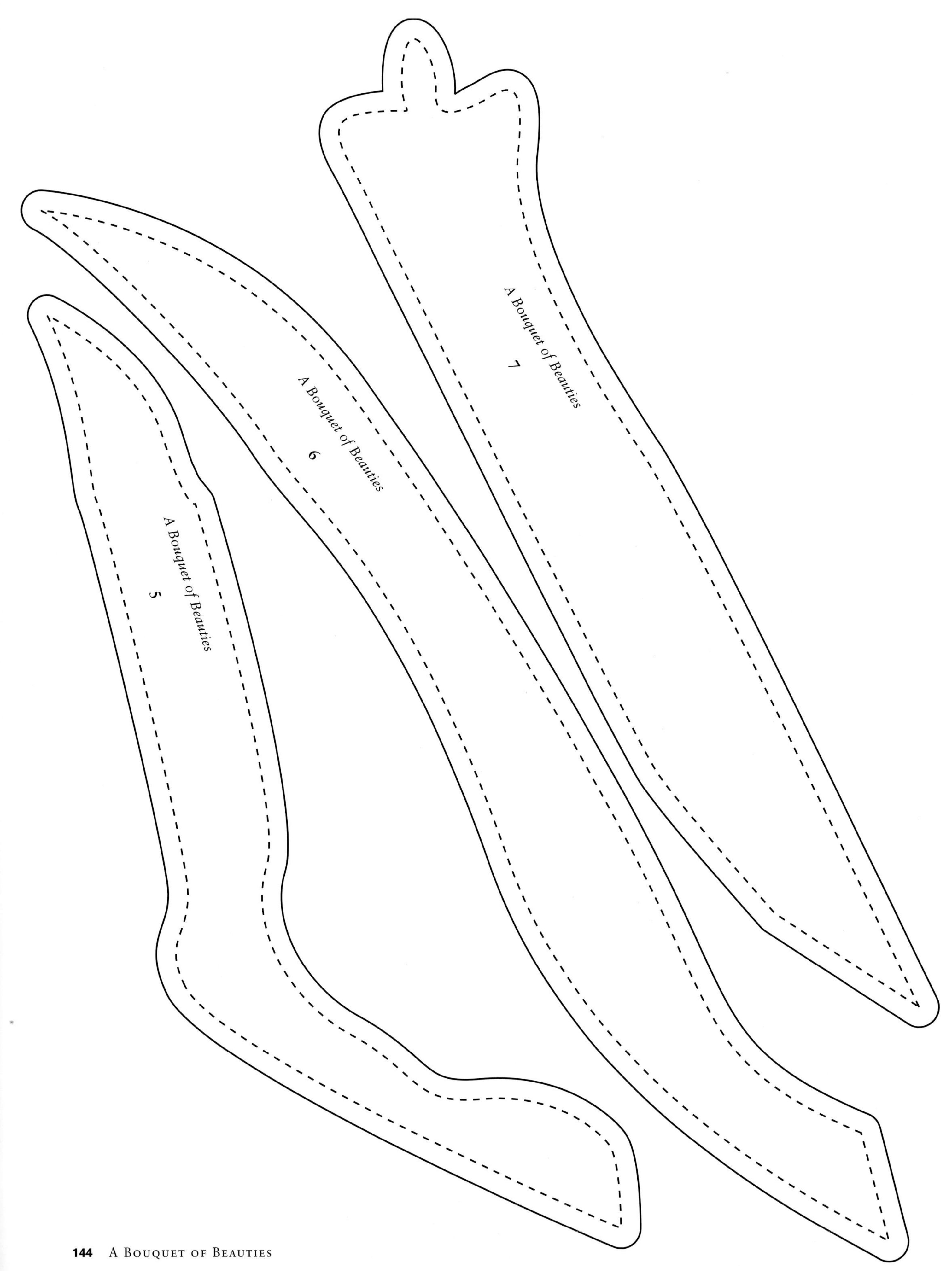
A Bouquet of Beauties
7
A Bouquet of Beauties
6
A Bouquet of Beauties
5

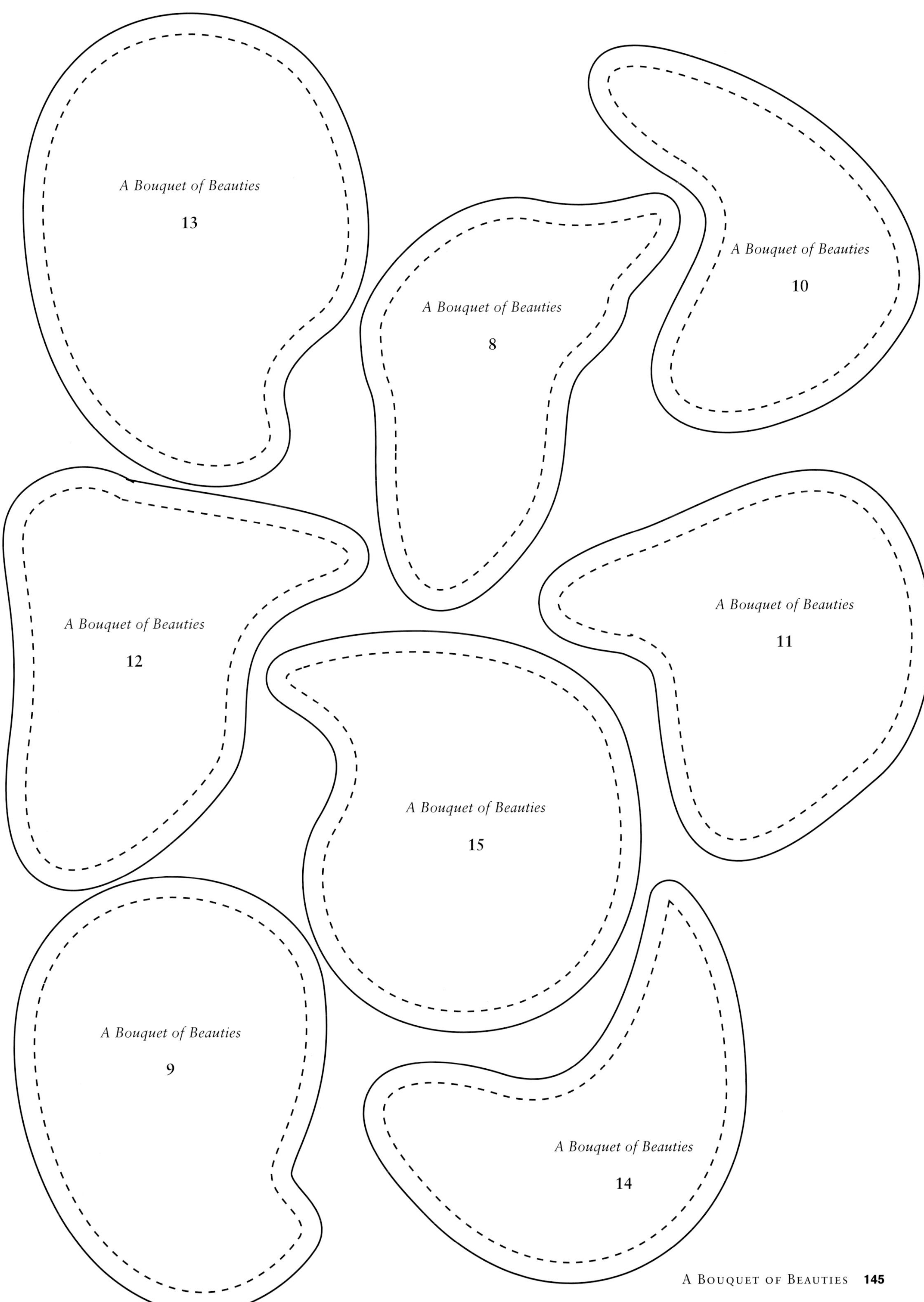
A Bouquet of Beauties
13
A Bouquet of Beauties
10
A Bouquet of Beauties
8
A Bouquet of Beauties
12
A Bouquet of Beauties
11
A Bouquet of Beauties
15
A Bouquet of Beauties
9
A Bouquet of Beauties
14

Biographies

Joyce R. Becker
A quilt maker of seventeen years, Joyce is particularly interested in the promotion of quilt making and in educating the public about quilting as an art form. Her greatest accomplishment in quilting has been overcoming fear and discovering new creative depths. She enjoys volunteering within the quilting community and writing about other quilters.

Flo Burghardt
In the past five years, Flo has progressed from making one-pattern quilts to making Baltimore Album quilts, beginning with simple wall quilts to a queen-size beauty. She was the Registration Chairman for the 1994 Great Pacific Northwest Quilt Show.

Rosy Carolan
A twenty year veteran, Rosy has recently stretched her quilting skills by taking creative risks. A frequent volunteer supporting events in the quilting community, her slide presentation, "Quilts as a Political, Social and Patriotic Statement," is given at no charge to local organizations.

Sheila R. Chapman
A quilt teacher and lecturer, Sheila has been quilting for seven years. Design is Sheila's favorite part of quilt making, to which she brings a strong technical background. Her work has been shown in local and juried regional shows and her quilts are exhibited in private collections.

Melody Crust
Melody is an accomplished, award-winning quilter whose work is exhibited internationally. She publishes a line of quilt labels and is a co-founder and vice president for The Association of Pacific Northwest Quilters. Melody also teaches and lectures.

Patti Cunningham
Best known for her award winning, original quilt designs, Patti has been quilting for 15 years. She lectures and demonstrates quilting throughout her community for schools, women's organizations, and guilds. She serves as guild president and is a board member of The Association of Pacific Northwest Quilters.

Karen Schoepflin Hagen
Karen loves to share the joys of quilting with others, so she tours each summer, taking her traveling exhibit to as many cities as possible. One day she hopes to house her legacy in her own quilt museum. She has been quilting since 1975.

Karla Harris
Confidence with fabric—putting anything together that fills the need of the moment—is the key to success for this quilter of eleven years. A quilting teacher, Karla loves interacting with her students. She was the featured artist at the 1995 Washington State Quilters Quilt Show and her award-winning work has been published widely.

Elizabeth Hendricks
Influenced by the movement and reflection of light aboard her house-barge home, Elizabeth began quilting in 1991. Her sensitive and personal pieces have appeared in publications and exhibitions throughout the country. Her best-known quilt, "Woman in a Box" has won many prestigious competitions.

Jane Herbst
Trained as a medical and natural science illustrator, Jane explores in her works her interest in biology and nature. A celebrated and award-winning textile artist, Jane finds opportunities for self-expression and creativity in fiber, regardless of the medium.

Connie James
Connie has always loved working with fabric and has been quilting since *1991*. An award-winning quilter, she looks for excitement, beauty, and fun in every quilt she makes.

Jeanne Nelson Loy
A firm believer in sharing what she has learned, Jeanne receives rave reviews from students in her crazy quilting class, "An Easy Way to Go Crazy." Jeanne believes in being exact in her work so finished pieces are both technically satisfying and artistically pleasing. She frequently judges quilt shows and volunteers within the quilting community.

Kathy Martin

After years of making scrap quilts, Kathy discovered art quilts and instantly knew she wanted to create quilt designs of her own. Her first attempt in this medium won a first-place ribbon and confirmed that she had finally found her own quilting niche.

Ree Nancarrow

A quilter of only three years, Ree has a thirty year background in fine arts. Living in Denali Park, Alaska, she has endless sources of inspiration for her quilts. Active throughout the Alaska quilting community, Ree teaches, lectures, and takes part in national and international competitions.

Kathleen M. O'Hanlon

A self-taught quilter, Kathleen began quilting in 1986, studying the works of other quilters, past and present, analyzing designs, patterns and palettes. Kathleen serves on the board of The Contemporary Quilt Art Association, with which she co-authored "Skills from School in Art," a curriculum guide for grades K-12 that seeks to integrate quilts into the classroom.

Barbara Lee Olson

Barbara lectures and teaches throughout Montana, educating the public through her presentation, "Art Quilts—The Creative Journey." She has won numerous ribbons in competitions and received a Judges Choice Award for Village Sunrise at the AIQA International Quilt Festival, 1994.

Karen Perrine

A fabric dyer of twenty years, Karen's quilting roots extend to her childhood days on a farm. Self-taught in surface design, her research delves into the myriad possibilities of applying color to cloth with paint, print, dye, and embroidery. Karen won an Award of Excellence at Quilt National 1995.

Charlene Phinney

Active in the quilting community for over twenty years, Charlene's quilting roots reach back to her childhood, when she played under her Grandmother McVicker's quilting frame. When lecturing, Charlene's special interest is how to let go and let the fabric take over.

Roslyn Rowley-Penk

A self-taught quilter of eight years, Ros is most proud of the quilts she makes for her children to keep them warm and cozy at night. She hopes the charity quilts she has made give those who might need it an extra hug. An active volunteer, Ros is a quilt teacher and is currently writing a book on quilting.

Brenda Duncan Shornick

Fortunate to grow up with a quilting tradition in a small community, Brenda learned early on from her mother to value needle arts and the women who practice them. Although she spent her working career in medical research, Brenda has not found anything as rewarding or as fulfilling as quilting.

Heather W. Tewell

A quilter of twenty years, each successive quilt Heather makes is an exploration into the possibilities of construction and design. Active throughout the Northwest as a quilt judge and as president and founder of The Association of Pacific Northwest Quilters, her work has won local and national awards.

Ivy Tuttle

Ivy began quilting in 1973 when she reluctantly took a quilting class with her sister. Ivy was hooked, her sister wasn't. Applique is Ivy's art form, and she particularly enjoys making pictorial quilts. Most of Ivy's quilts have been given away to family and friends.

Deborah White

Debbie began quilting in 1982 as a creative outlet. She specializes in miniatures, and designs, teaches, lectures, and is writing a book on this quilting form. Entering competitions drives her to accomplish things she would not otherwise attempt, and one of her greatest achievements so far is a second-place ribbon at the 1995 AQS Show.

Resources

The following Quilt Digest Press books supply the technical information needed for basic quilt making.

Quilts! Quilts!! Quilts!!! by Diana McClun and Laura Nownes
Quilt's Galore! by Diana McClun and Laura Nownes
Appliqué! Appliqué!! Appliqué!!! by Laurene Sinema

Be sure to read the chapters regarding fabric, batting, backing, quilting, and binding. In most cases, I recommend you use prewashed, 100 percent cotton fabrics for your art.

Many of the artists here have used specific products in their quilt art. I have tried to list as many of these products as possible so that you too might be able to experiment, grow, and discover! Ask your local fabric and quilt shops if they can order these products for you.

River Rocks

Cotton sateen fabric, white, ready to dye
Testfabrics, Inc.
Middlesex, NJ

Procion MxTM dye
Pro Chemical & Dye, Inc.
Somerset, MA

Dharma Trading Co.
San Rafael, CA

Createx Fabric Pigment
Createx Colors
East Granby, CT

Lumiere and Neopaque Fabric Pigment
Textile Colors
Riverdale, MD

Metallic Knit Mesh for leaves
Jehlor Fantasy Fabrics
Seattle, WA

Specialized threads
Sulky metallic and rayon threads

Fox Pond and Mostly Lichens

The boiling water soluble stabilizer used is not available in this country. A good substitute is Melt Away™ by Madeira

Wild Flowers at Mt. Rainier and Stars at Ocean Shores

Hot Fix Stones™ & Hot Knife (sparkling stars in the sky)
Jehlor Fantasy Fabrics
Seattle, WA

Wild Flowers at Mt. Rainier

Procion Mx™ dyes, listed above

Midnight Sun and The Stardusters in Their Night Garden

Pattern paper (48″ or 66″ widths)
Mill End Store
Beaverton, OR

Further Reference

Flynn, John, *Step by Step Trapunto and Stippling* (Billings, MT: Flynn Quilt Frame Company, 1992).

Horton, Roberta, *Calico and Beyond* (Lafayette, CA: C&T Publishing, 1986).

Johnston, Ann, *Dye Painting* (Paducah, KY: American Quilter's Society, 1992).

Magaret, Pat M., and Donna I. Slusser, *Watercolor Quilts* (Bothell, WA: That Patchwork Place, 1993).

Schneider, Sally, *Painless Borders* (Bothell, WA: That Patchwork Place, 1992).

Sienkiewicz, Elly, *Spoken Without a Word* (Washington, D.C.: The Turtle Hill Press, 1983).